MOTHER DAUGHTER SISTER BRIDE
rituals of womanhood

MOTHER DAUGHTER SISTER BRIDE

rituals of womanhood

Joanne B. Eicher   Lisa Ling

NATIONAL GEOGRAPHIC

Washington, D. C.

Contents

Previous page: A geisha in Kyoto, Japan. Opposite: A young girl playing dress-up. Following pages: A ritual bath during a voodoo pilgrimage in Haiti. Pages 8–9: Getting ready for a fashion show. Pages 10–11: A swimsuit contest in the early 1920s. Pages 12–13: An Indian bride with a traditional nose ring. Pages: 14–15: A weary bride and groom. Pages 24–25: Carnival in Venice. Pages 26–27: A Bulgarian mother grieving for her murdered son in 1980.

Generation to Generation

Introduction by Joanne B. Eicher

MOTHERS, DAUGHTERS, SISTERS, AND BRIDES. SIMILAR ROLES EXIST AROUND THE WORLD, BUT DIFFERENT CULTURAL EXPECTATIONS MEAN DIFFERENT INTERPRETATIONS AND DIFFERENT RITUALS WHEN CHANGING FROM ONE POSITION IN LIFE TO ANOTHER. THE IMAGES AND TEXT IN THIS BOOK REPRESENT IDEAS ABOUT RITUAL PROCESSES PRACTICED BY WOMEN AND GIRLS EVERYWHERE. RITUALS, CULTURALLY CREATED AND EXPECTED PATTERNS OF BEHAVIOR, ARE LEARNED AND TRANSMITTED FROM GENERATION TO GENERATION, ORDINARILY WITHIN A TRANSCRIBED SPACE AND TIME. THE NAMES OF THESE RITUAL PATTERNS INDICATE ETHNIC, TRIBAL, RELIGIOUS, GEOGRAPHIC, OR NATIONAL IDENTITY, SUCH AS CHRISTIAN BAPTISM, BUDDHIST CONTEMPLATION, SANDE INITIATION IN SIERRA LEONE, OR MISS AMERICA PAGEANT. THE STUDY OF RITUALS BEGAN WHEN EARLY ANTHROPOLOGISTS FOUND THE BEHAVIOR OF PEOPLE IN DISTANT LOCATIONS FASCINATING, EVEN PECULIAR, ESPECIALLY BEHAVIOR IN EXOTIC RELIGIOUS PRACTICES THAT WERE SOCIALLY AND PHYSICALLY REMOTE FROM

A Dutch mother in Friesland rocks her baby to sleep in a cradle that has been handed down through generations.

the scholars' own experience. They collected information firsthand, hoping to explain ritual behavior.

In the early 1900s, French ethnographer Arnold van Gennep observed that ritual behavior developed when a person passed from one social state, such as that of a girl, to another, that of a woman. He called these rituals "rites of passage," proposing three phases: separation from the old position, transition from old to new, and incorporation into the new. Such rites of passage occur for a single individual at a specific time, such as individual baptism, or for several individuals at the same time, such as a sorority initiation.

Another type of ritual, known as a rite of intensification or calendrical rite (occurring annually at a prescribed time), takes place when group members engage in ritual behavior that reaffirms, and thus intensifies, commitment to an identity with their group. These rituals focus on group identity, such as Fourth of July celebrations and parades in the United States to celebrate independence from Great Britain.

Critical in all rituals is dressing the body. This involves all five senses as we modify or add to our bodies. Dress as significant and effective communication usually provides the first signal of a ritual process. Selecting and wearing appropriate ritual dress becomes required and integrally associated with the ritual. Common rites of passage the world over relate to biological processes; these include birth, childhood, adolescence, adulthood, and death. Each biological change may launch a social change. As a girl's body develops physically, initiation ceremonies and marriage celebrations serve to indicate the transition from being a girl, a single female, to being a mature, adult woman. Rituals of baptism and confirmation are rites of passage, but can also be rites of intensification that celebrate an individual's membership in a religious group, affirmed by the religious group.

As researchers moved their sites of fieldwork closer to home, they realized that practices from afar are neither as exotic nor as different from their own practices as they once thought. Curiosity about rituals evolved into a desire for more comprehensive knowledge. By the end of the 1800s Western scholars had developed a new discipline of study called anthropology, the "science of man," to understand how other people lived.

The performance of community rituals connected to religion and rites of passage particularly attracted the attention of anthropologists. Explorers, missionaries, and other travelers had earlier described unfamiliar people, living in unfamiliar places, celebrating life in unfamiliar ways. Nineteenth-century scholars in America and Europe wanted more than descriptions; they wanted to analyze the significance of the rituals.

Charles Darwin's ideas of biological evolution and "survival of the fittest" influenced them in particular; they perceived his ideas useful to analyze social life. Anthropologists declared that social evolution paralleled biological evolution and that it explained social hierarchy among human groups.

People being observed often used rudimentary tools, wore few if any clothes, and exhibited "strange" ways of being a child, becoming an adult, taking a mate, rearing a family, and acknowledging death. The observers declared their own ways of life as advanced; they believed themselves superior, at the top of the social evolutionary ladder. In addition, many of these early scholars were men who often downplayed or paid scant attention to women's roles and rituals.

In the 21st century, scholarly knowledge has crushed beliefs about social evolution and also uncovered the significance of women's roles. Social and biological evidence document that healthy human beings, no matter what gender, skin color, height, or weight, all possess similar capacities: They learn to speak a language, to relate to other human beings in friendship and in love, and to create patterns of behavior that are passed down as rituals through the generations.

In this book, we focus on rituals related to community, family, sisterhood, and the self and present cross-cultural examples. A common Western example illustrates van Gennep's three phases of ritual practice: A bride-to-be may purchase not only her white wedding dress but also a trousseau that includes a going-away outfit and a negligee ensemble for her wedding night. The white wedding dress signifies virginity as she departs from her family; the going-away outfit represents her transition from unmarried, virginal woman to wife; and her negligee ensemble emphasizes incorporation into her new family as a socially defined sexual being, a wife.

⌒

Some ritual behavior does not represent a full-fledged rite of passage, but instead is a ritualized practice. For example, many beauty practices among women involve a ritual that has been learned culturally. Some ritual practices are solitary and a part of daily life, as is the case when a woman dresses in the morning and applies cosmetics in a prescribed fashion. Although alone in the moment, she follows a set procedure, one probably learned from her mother, sisters, and female friends. Some beauty practices involve family interaction when a mother teaches her daughter to wash and brush her hair. Still other practices exemplify sisterhood, when women bathe together in a Turkish *hammam*—a communal bathhouse—or a Finnish sauna. Finally, a beauty practice may be found within the community when women tan together on a public beach.

Rites of passage are associated with individuals, but calendrical rites are community rituals that focus on community integration, such as the religious and political holidays Christmas, Eid el Fitr, Independence Day, and Passover. National beauty contests are another example. Ritual behavior in these cases requires special dress or costuming. Special foods may also play a part, with women preparing dishes, serving, and cleaning up.

Anthropologists first believed that ritual practices found in remote places changed little and were followed stringently. For example, anthropologist Ina Corrine Brown supported the idea of social stability in remote places when she reported in 1963: "The Balinese term for time before the coming of the white man is 'when the world was steady.'"

Anthropologists also thought that industrial societies possessed few rituals in comparison to small, compact cultures. Over time, they discarded both beliefs. In fact, change occurs everywhere, sometimes fast and sometimes slow. Industrialized societies may lack rituals parallel to small societies, but they have developed their own. For instance, graduates from secondary school or university wearing a graduation gown celebrate their coming of age just as adolescent initiates elsewhere celebrate coming of age with special hairdos or body paint. Both emphasize being launched into the world of adults.

Rituals around the world involve both men and women. We focus here on women's roles in rituals and women's special ritual practices, looking both at familiar and unfamiliar examples and highlighting some changing practices. When reading and thinking about the rituals of others, we should remember that anthropologists find not only the rituals of others exotic, but also our own. Generally, we believe our own rituals to be "normal." We human beings are all exotic, depending on whose point of view is taken in deciding what behavior, what ritual, is exotic.

Emerging Rituals

Introduction by Lisa Ling

As a journalist I've had the privilege of reporting from more than 30 countries around the world. In my early 20s, I worked for Channel One News, broadcast to hundreds of middle- and high-school classrooms in the United States. My assignments took me to such places as Afghanistan, Iraq, Vietnam, and Kazakhstan. Most recently I have hosted the National Geographic Channel's flagship series, *EXPLORER*, and I am a special contributor to the *OPRAH WINFREY SHOW*. Both of these jobs also send me to report on varied cultures. In my travels, I've observed longstanding rituals such as the *QUINCEAÑERA* celebrations in Mexico to usher 15-year-old girls to womanhood; the stringing of mango leaves at the entrance of a Kashmiri home to announce a wedding; and the celebration of Saints Peter and Paul Day in Russia, when children play tricks on villagers on the eve of July 12. Rituals are created within cultures and imparted to

Dressed to impress, a woman uses her looks to attract the attention of possible "mates."

generations throughout time. As the world changes, old rituals change with the times, and new rituals are established. I have witnessed practices emerging among particular ethnic groups that are distinctively unique to their respective communities. For example, when hundreds of young Colombian girls are forced, or willingly leave their families, to join the armed rebel movements, they inevitably establish new rituals within their new families. Away from the mainstream, they form an unusual sisterhood and cultivate new rituals. These activities are independent of anything they have done or experienced in their previous lives.

In Iran, scores of young women, who are required to abide by *sharia*—Islamic law—to cover their entire body with a long loose-fitting robe and a headscarf, are finding new ways to challenge the status quo. They are collectively, but subtly, enhancing their appearance and, in the process, making a daring statement. Here, large numbers of young women are amending strict cultural rituals and bravely creating their own.

In Japan, record numbers of women are choosing not to get married and remain single. Though Japan is considered one of the most industrialized nations in the world, its women are somewhat marginalized. As housewives, many women have cold relationships with their spouse, because the husband spends little time at home. More and more women are choosing to forego such lives of domesticity and remain in the workplace with the hope of ascending to higher professional levels.

Here, the rituals involving marriage and raising children are challenged by new rituals involving the self. In focusing on the self, these women are inspiring other women to follow suit. A Japanese woman in her 30s told me that she admired American and European women who are not defined by having a husband and family. As one result of many women's decision not to marry and have children, Japan is experiencing a serious negative population growth. Presently, Japan has one of the lowest birth rates in the world, 1.3 children per woman, as compared to the birth rate in the United States, at 2.034 children per woman.

Rituals surrounding beautification seem to transcend time and culture. Whether force-feeding young girls in Mauritania to fatten them to ideal size, or letting girls diet to model-slimness in the United States, every country and culture has its own definition of beauty. In some cases, with the help of advances in medicine, women are changing their appearance so drastically that they no longer look like they belong to the culture from which they come. Cosmetic surgery is rampant. Many women who have tried it have difficulty stopping and keep finding new procedures.

⟳

There are few stages in a woman's life—no matter where in the world she lives—as symbolic as marriage. Rituals such as bridal showers and honeymoons precede and follow wedding festivities. A wedding celebration signals the next phase in a couple's relationship. In many cultures, a dowry payment is expected upon consummation of a marriage.

In India, although the traditional ritual of giving dowry has been outlawed since 1961, there is an unwritten rule that obligates the bride's family to pay money or make a material gift, such as a dishwasher, a car, or a microwave oven, if a wedding is to go forward. For decades this illegal practice continued, and more recently, despite India's unprecedented economic growth, it still prevails. The ritual of giving dowry sometimes turns deadly for those women whose families are unable to meet the demands. An estimated 6,000 women a year—

out of a population of more than one billion—suffer dire, usually fatal, consequences for their family's inability to honor excessive dowry demands.

Sometimes rituals evolve as a result of something that happens in an entirely different culture—on the other side of the planet. I traveled with an American couple from Atlanta, Georgia, halfway around the world to meet a new addition to their family. They went to mainland China with other American couples to adopt a Chinese baby girl. In their case, the traditional rituals surrounding the birth of a baby did not apply: no Lamaze classes or trips to the doctor's office for ultrasounds or sonograms. The babies who joined these American families were not even of a similar racial or cultural background. Nonetheless, new rituals emerged that pertained to the families engaging in the adoption process. All of the couples had to fill out the same forms and wait for a long time for the adoption process to go through. And all of the couples came back to the United States with a new member of their family, more knowledgeable about a different culture and resolved to blend customs and rituals for the child.

When an entire culture feels oppressed by another, drastic and often deadly measures will be employed to make the loudest, most powerful statement possible. This is the case in the Occupied Territories of Israel. Thousands of Palestinians have been killed in the decades-old conflict. They are known to their people as martyrs, and their glorification is akin to hero worship. Many in the Palestinian territories feel that the only way to resist and fight the Israeli Army is to use their own bodies as weapons. Suicide bombing has become synonymous with the struggle in the Middle East, and the practice has spread around the world. Today, hardly a week goes by without news of a suicide bombing somewhere in the world. The practice has become a ritual of one community in its stand against another.

For immigrant families, time-honored rituals can change drastically when it is inconvenient to hold on to old customs, and there is little or no community support. Their old traditions have to keep pace with life in the new country, and are modified accordingly.

Immigration also upsets communities left behind. In the summer of 2004, I visited rural towns in the state of Oaxaca in Mexico, while working on a documentary about illegal immigration from Mexico to the U.S. for National Geographic's *Explorer*. I found large populations of women, with few men. When I inquired about the disparity, I was told that it was because so many men had left for America to find work. Entire homes had been boarded up and abandoned. I stayed in the home of a 17-year-old girl named Itika, who in a few days was going to try to cross the Mexico/U.S. border with her uncle, his wife, and a younger brother. It took Itika and her family three days to cross. Finally on American soil, they were picked up by a family member who drove them to work in a chicken plant in Heavner, Oklahoma. That day they joined the estimated 400,000 Mexicans who leave their country annually for work in the United States.

The women who are left behind must often deal with a house full of children and in-laws; whatever support they do get comes from other women. Because of the loss of men, women have to assume new responsibilities. They have to abbreviate rituals or develop new ones because they are absorbed in working the fields, in taking care of livestock, and in doing other types of manual labor that was once reserved for their men.

I am often sent to cover women's issues, and I record not only women's sadness and suffering, but also their resilience. My work has been consumed by such stories, and I continue to see how women cope and resort to practices that evolve into new rituals.

Community

THE ANNUAL HMONG NEW YEAR FESTIVAL IN MINNEAPOLIS AND ST. PAUL (KNOWN AS THE TWIN CITIES) BEGINS AS A ROW OF YOUNG MEN AND A ROW OF YOUNG WOMEN FACING EACH OTHER THROW SMALL CROCHETED BALLS BACK AND FORTH. ALTHOUGH IN THEIR ANCESTRAL HOME IN THAILAND AND LAOS,

they recited and exchanged lines of poetry as well as balls, in the United States they exchange flirtatious looks, giggles, and smiles.

The Hmong now living in Minnesota provide a colorful example of a courtship ritual embedded in the community. They brought their custom of ball tossing from their homes and refugee camps in Southeast Asia. Courtship rituals are diverse globally, but all precede wedding rituals and represent part of the departure ritual from one's family. The New Year events attract Hmong youths and adults, who attend from all parts of the United States as a way of meeting a future mate through an accepted cultural practice.

The young women are decked out in elaborate outfits that include a hat or turban, a blouse and skirt ensemble, and fashionable shoes worn with leggings or pantyhose. Often the young men also wear colorful trousers and vests, but the women remain the center of attention. The colors of their dresses range from bright pinks and blues to dark burgundy and black. Cross-stitching and reverse appliqué—traditional embellishment techniques—provide a dimension of texture and additional color. Heavy silver necklaces and coins sewn on the women's belts and men's vests add a further dimension of sound throughout the space of St. Paul's River Centre and Minneapolis's Metrodome.

At the Hounen fertility festival in Japan, women parade with phallus symbols to the Tagata shrine.

Women elders brought their skills of sewing and embroidering from Laos and Thailand to create the items of festive garb in the Twin Cities when they began to arrive after 1975. The longer the Hmong live in the Twin Cities, however, the more often vendors bring imported items from China and Laos to replace the home-sewn garments, for young Hmong women have not taken up the tradition of sewing. The sewing skills taught by elder women in a family to ready their daughters for courtship, to sponsor their imminent departure for marriage, are rarely taught to the young ones in the United States because they attend public schools. Little time remains for young women to learn the skills of intricate handiwork. Older women still produce some of the garments, but in many families, additional items must be purchased to complete the special outfit. Thus, the place of the family in organizing resources to launch a daughter into marriage has begun to shift from providing domestic skills to providing cash to purchase items in the marketplace.

Visitors who observed the ball-tossing event over the course of several years soon realized that Hmong fashion changes from year to year. New styles replace earlier ones. This fact comes as a surprise to outsiders, who think that "traditional dress" does not change and becomes stuck in the past. The young women most often choose to wear currently fashionable footwear, such as extreme platform shoes when they were in style, a design the short Hmong women liked particularly well because the shoes made them look taller.

Drastic changes often occur in the details on garments and types of headgear. For example, in the 1980s and 1990s young women found wearing the traditional wrapped turban uncomfortable. When getting dressed, they had to kneel in front of an older woman, a mother or an aunt, who wrapped 14 yards of fabric around their head to fashion the turban, and the turban flattened the hairdo underneath. Few women wear these turbans anymore. Instead they buy a prewrapped turban that can be worn like a hat.

Over the past few years, vendors have also imported hats of different styles from Laos and China, some with wide brims and beaded dangles, some with brightly colored pink and green feathers, others with sequins. They are now beginning to import skirts made from machine-printed cotton that imitates brightly colored embroidery. These skirts present a popular and less expensive alternative to skirts with the time-consuming handi-

PUBLIC KNOWLEDGE THAT THE INDIVIDUAL HAS SUCCESSFULLY MADE THE TRANSITION FROM ONE SOCIAL POSITION TO ANOTHER HELPS THE INDIVIDUAL ASSUME THE NEW ROLE.

work formerly expected on a young woman's outfit. In these cases, the importance of special dress for the Hmong New Year celebration continues even though form and details of the dress change. The purpose of the ritual, to provide an opportunity for courtship, remains intact, and the public witnessing of courtship in the Hmong community underscores the importance of community affirmation. Meeting members of the opposite sex and finding a potential marriage partner is an occasion that is played out as community members watch and affirm this purpose.

Many rites of passage require affirmation by the community as a central aspect. Public knowledge that the individual or group of individuals has successfully made the transition from one social position to another helps the individual assume the new role. Weddings. Initiations. Debutante balls. Funerals. What roles do women play in these events across the globe? How are these roles carried out? What interaction occurs between the community members who attend the events and the women involved?

Across cultures, wedding and marriage rituals, ceremonies critical in the lives of women, involve sequences of expected behavior for their rites of passage, performed before members of the community. These rites of passage most often involve three phases, as outlined by French anthropologist Arnold van Gennep: departure, transition, and incorporation.

The crux of marriage as a concept, especially in many non-Western societies, is connecting the families of the betrothed couple. The family of the bride relinquishes her to the groom and his family, resulting in the bride's position in life changing more markedly than the groom's. She leaves the role of being a single woman and changes to being a wife. Focus centers on her, with attention paid to her wedding garments, jewelry, and even the dowry that she takes with her into her new position. The dowry can be money or other gifts from her family as she departs from them. Her appearance at the ceremony as the bride is often the apotheosis of the event, whether she is shielded from view of the groom and guests by a particular item of apparel, such as a veil, or whether she is paraded in splendor for all guests to see. Rites of passage for marriage may spread over several days or weeks, sometimes even months, with many parts of the community involved at specific times for specific events. Depending on the societal value attached to being defined as virginal or sexually enticing, the color and style of her items of apparel become meaningful and symbolic.

In the United States and Europe in the early and mid-1900s, a bride in a formal, white wedding gown often wore a veil that covered her face until the vows were completed. At that point, the groom lifted the veil from her face to let it fall over her back. This tradition emphasized her departure from her family and the dissolution of a barrier between her and her husband. Similarly, when a Korean bride wears a traditional gown, she raises her arms and hands to cover her face with the wide sleeves of her gown to hide her face from her groom and the guests.

In contrast, in many contemporary weddings in the United States, the bride's gown, even if white, may no longer emphasize modesty and purity, for brides often display themselves in wedding gowns with revealing features: low décolletage, bare shoulders, and a form-fitting silhouette. Few now cover their face with a veil, but instead only drape the veil over their head to float down the back of the gown. Changes in dress may be a sign of the changes in underwriting the wedding expenses; in many cases, the couple being married share or shoulder the costs completely. Shifting the responsibility for financing the ceremony indicates the release of the bride from the tether of her family, just as the change in her wedding ensemble implies.

Debutante balls and related parties represent another variation of courtship ritual, for the original point was the formal introduction of a daughter to friends and family. The origin of the idea of a formal introduction stems from the French word *debut* meaning "first appearance," or entering into society. The custom was adopted by Queen Charlotte of England, in the late 1700s, to introduce young women from noble society to the court as a way to meet the families of eligible young men. Dress requirements were later instituted, including the proper length of dress, specified colors, and appropriate gloves and accessories. The idea traveled across the Atlantic Ocean to the United States, where upper-class families held small parties for the same purpose. Many variations of the debut have occurred since then. Small parties sponsored by the family grew into large, extravagant, and exclusive balls for a group of women from similar elite backgrounds. Charity balls also allowed middle-class daughters to participate in such public spectacles.

In the 21st century, presentation of young women to the community varies by region and by cultural group across the world. In the United States, in San Antonio, Texas, during Fiesta Week, the young women to be presented are selected as duchesses, a princess, and a queen, all who wear gowns of rhinestone glitter and opulence that represent a designated theme. Michaele Haynes, curator of the Witte Museum in San Antonio, reports that Fiesta Week captures all three of van Gennep's tripartite elements of ritual, for the group of young women who have been selected are separated in time and in physical and social space from their families as they prepare for the ball. The ball illustrates transition, and after the ball, the young women are incorporated as adult members of the community.

In another example, among Latino families in the United States, the *quinceañera*, the 15th birthday celebration, launches the 15-year-old daughter into adulthood. On her special day, she wears a pastel-colored or white floor-length ball gown, similar to a bridal gown. She may first attend Mass, acknowledging her Catholic religious beliefs and pledging her chastity. Following the Mass, her mother, or father, presents her with a pair of high-heeled shoes as an emblem of maturity to replace her girlish flat-soled shoes. An elaborate party follows, a reception for her community-at-large, which witnesses her coming of age. A court of female friends in similar festive attire accompanies her, and young men dressed in tuxedos escort them.

Along the same lines, African-American debutante balls allow recognition of young women's maturation into adulthood. Annette Lynch of the University of Northern Iowa reports in her research in Waterloo, Iowa, that women community leaders initiated the idea that participation by young women should rest on their significant social and academic accomplishments rather than their family backgrounds. Proceeds from the sale of tickets flow into a scholarship fund. Success of the annual event has become evident as attendance has grown, aided not only by interest in the African-American community, but also by the organizers' determination to keep the cost of tickets low so friends and neighbors can witness the event. Debutante balls contrast with quinceañeras, for in the former, a group of debutantes are presented simultaneously to the audience rather than just one, as in the latter.

Initiation rituals for women that are followed by presentation to the community at large occur in many places around the world.

In Africa, among the Mende people of Sierra Leone, girls are separated for initiation purposes from the rest of the community, usually in a sheltered place in the forest, to be taught "the secrets of womanhood." With the help of adult women, they become prepared physically and mentally for their new role, learning "beauty, grace, and self-control," all of which they will need within the multigenerational, polygamous households of their future husbands. The initiates are covered with white clay during the transition period as prelude for the rituals, which include clitoridectomy. This surgical procedure, although controversial to many people outside Mende culture, is deemed necessary among the Mende to mark the transition from child to adult.

When the initiation ceremonies are over, the initiates are presented to the community as fully mature women. The initiation period provided a sanctuary for them to leave childhood behind and undergo transformation to womanhood, before becoming incorporated into the community which acknowledges their new status as women.

A significant part of the presentation ritual is that the women's association members dance with carved, wooden masks, an unusual feature because in any other region of Africa, only the men dance wearing this type of mask. The women's society is known as Sande, and

INITIATION RITUALS FOR WOMEN
THAT ARE FOLLOWED BY PRESENTATION TO THE
COMMUNITY AT LARGE OCCUR IN MANY
PLACES AROUND THE WORLD.

their masks are distinctively carved with encircling ridges at the neck, said to represent the ripples that form when an individual surfaces from the water of a river or a pool into which she dreamed she has plunged after dancing successfully.

Members of the community loom large in marriage and coming-of-age rituals as represented by presentation balls and initiation ceremonies. Formal nuptials and big balls take place under the watch of invited family members and friends, a group of well-wishers that may result in a guest list of several hundred people. Notable for long guest lists are weddings of the well-to-do in India. The act of attendance by friends, neighbors, and family members recognizes the significance of the

bride's transition to wife-hood. For many community members, whether family or not, rites of passage bring various people together, who may not have been in direct contact with each other for some time. Weddings, debutante balls, and funerals serve as events for community gatherings, affirming a specific rite of passage for an individual.

In the case of funerals, the rites of passage also clearly represent departure, transition, and incorporation; the deceased leave their families behind, and the community gathers to honor the life and mourn the loss of the deceased. A combination of the way in which the deceased is dressed and the specifics of the ceremony indicate the ritual phase. For example, the cultural expectation for dressing the body emphasizes which phase is involved. If the deceased is dressed in her own clothing, the departure from everyday life is stressed, which is the case in many Christian funerals. A hospice nurse in California told me that it was common for terminally ill patients in her care, particularly women, to indicate either to her or to some family member in her presence the clothing they wanted to wear in the casket. They firmly asked to be laid out as they saw themselves and as they wanted to be remembered by their friends and family when viewed.

In other cultures, community members emphasize the transition of a deceased female into the afterlife by requiring the body to be dressed in a shroud.

Such is the case in Korea, where natural-colored ramie fibers are used to make the shroud for both women and men, because Koreans expect the garment to disintegrate along with the body. In addition, the color denotes the somber occasion and helps set the mood for the mourners. Social activities, however, are an integral part of the mourning process, for the family members are expected to stay up all night, and their friends join them to eat and play cards to ease the pain of mourning and help pass the time.

My research in Nigeria on funerals among the Kalabari people of the Niger Delta area portrays an extensive network of support from several corners of the community. Female relatives dress the corpse of a woman as she lies in state within the family home and is moved from bed to bed and room to room. When she is moved, the women change her garments. They dress her in fine Kalabari clothing, a wrapper, blouse, and head tie, but for her final garment, if she is Christian, they select a special gown made of white eyelet or lace to symbolize her Christian belief and her incorporation in the afterlife of heaven.

After her interment, community members honor her memory and salute the extended family members during the following week by visiting the rooms with the beds where she has lain, which are subsequently decorated with a wide variety of fabrics. Members from the extended family, the women who are in charge of taking care of precious family textiles, lend the textiles from the family cache of treasured cloth after an individual has died or from their own wardrobe of wrappers. Female relatives fold them on the bed in clever shapes, resembling giant and colorful fabric origami, providing a setting for a "fitting farewell."

Birth and death are closely intertwined because as a member of one generation passes on, the relatives and friends in the community focus attention on the next generation, the babies and children who attend the funeral events. The community becomes formally involved as participant in acknowledging the arrival of the newly born and young in such cases as baptisms, christenings, and naming ceremonies. Again, the dress of the infant is often a paramount issue. In the case of a child being baptized in a Greek Orthodox church, all items put on the child's body must be new and never before worn.

Traditions may change, however. Past practice among Christian families was dressing an infant for baptism in an heirloom christening gown, taking pride in owning a gown handed down through several generations. In the 21st century, though, some parents reject the idea of a "gown" for a boy baby and believe it should be a garment reserved for girls.

Among the Kalabari people, a new mother is sequestered for a period of days following the child's birth; then, if she is Christian, she will march in proces-

THE COMMUNITY BECOMES FORMALLY INVOLVED IN ACKNOWLEDGING THE ARRIVAL OF THE NEWLY BORN IN BAPTISMS, CHRISTENINGS, AND NAMING CEREMONIES.

sion with her baby and family to the church to be seated in the front row. During the service, the child is presented to the congregation and thereby incorporated into the community.

Within Kalabari tradition, however, the emphasis is on a woman becoming a new mother. During the sequestering period, she is pampered by being fed and bathed, and other family members care for her infant, only bringing the child to her for breast-feeding. At the end of this period, over a span of several days, the mother dresses in a series of elegant Kalabari textiles, wearing brightly colored madras plaids, striped silks, and embroidered velvets imported from India. Attired in these special garments, she parades through the town, going from compound to compound, sometimes stopping to dance, to display herself to the community. The baby does not accompany her. The community members affirm their recognition of her and express their appreciation for her new role by giving her gifts of money as she visits them.

The practice of national and international beauty pageants illustrates a rite of intensification and calendrical rite that caught on after its beginning in 1921 as the Miss America Pageant. The winner, selected from pageant finalists, represents the nation in regard to several qualities of femininity, including what is now termed as "being physically fit," shown by wearing a swimsuit. Other requirements demand proof of intelligence by having the contestant answer questions and exhibit talent by performing in the talent contest. The Miss America Foundation states that the primary focus of the pageant is not on beauty, but on opportunities to obtain an educational scholarship.

Today, the Miss America Pageant/Scholarship Program and the Miss USA Pageant—focused on beauty and preliminary to the Miss Universe Pageant—have the highest profile of some 7,500 pageants franchised annually. Many of these relate to commercial products and enterprises, like Miss Budweiser or Princess Kay of the Milky Way at the Minnesota State Fair, who has the likeness of her head carved in butter. In the Miss America Pageant, the winners, Miss America and her runners-up, receive significant scholarships to help them achieve their educational goals stated in the presence of a large, immediate community made up of the audience in front of them and a much larger television audience.

The history of the Miss America Pageant is fascinating. At its beginning as a bathing beauty contest in Atlantic City to stimulate tourism, the young contestants were representatives of WASP (White Anglo-Saxon Protestant) middle-class values, presenting an image of the dominant culture of the United States. Being single has continued as a firm requirement for entrants. The first and only Jewish winner (through 2004) was Bess Myerson in 1945, and the first black winner was Vanessa Williams in 1983, indicating a recognition of a more diverse population. Still, the winners of all of these contests, no matter what their color or heritage, represent idealized visions of femininity current at the time. Key to the history and description of these pageants is the judges' affirmation of community values regarding female beauty and deportment.

One source reporting on the growth and significance of beauty contests around the world declares "the idealized femininity put on stage in beauty contests is often closely associated with broader concepts such as morality, or with large social entities such as the 'nation.'" The writer further points out that beauty contests are not at all trivial, but instead, are important and complex events that serve to represent a nation and its status. Indeed, when two competitions (Miss World and Miss Universe) were each won by an Indian woman in 1994, an executive of the women's magazine *Femina* declared, "It's a victory for the nation. The Indian subcontinent has come into the limelight."

Community participation in rituals can be a key factor when community members witness role transformations of a young girl to a woman, or a woman without a child to a mother. Community members also take part in the approval and selection of beautiful young women to represent an ideal that reflects morality and femininity within a region or nation. The public nature of such events solidifies the roles enacted in the rites of passage or rites of intensification, providing a type of "glue" that makes the new role "stick," or the image of the nation more real.

SANTIAGO DE CUBA, CUBA / 1998

KYOTO, JAPAN / 1990

"A PEDESTAL IS AS MUCH A PRISON

AS ANY SMALL, CONFINED SPACE."

— GLORIA STEINEM

MADRID, SPAIN / 1986

CARNIVAL — a centuries-old annual celebration of life—liberates women, allowing them to forget their troubles and rejoice in their femaleness. /pages 36-37

DRESSED IN THE TRADITIONAL white *uchikake* bridal kimono worn for a private Shinto wedding ceremony, a bride displays herself to the community to receive their blessings and good wishes. /pages 38-39

SÃO PAULO, BRAZIL / 1987

A MOTHER HOSTS an elaborate event for friends and family following her daughter's christening, a naming ceremony that formally introduces the child into the church and to the social community. /above left

AFTER WITNESSING THE WEDDING ceremony, nominally giving their blessing and approval to the union, guests celebrate their friends' nuptials with food and drink. /above

BODY ORNAMENTATION often identifies a person's ethnic affiliation. In a custom no longer practiced and rarely seen today, women of the Sara people of Chad wore lip plates as a fertility symbol. /page 42

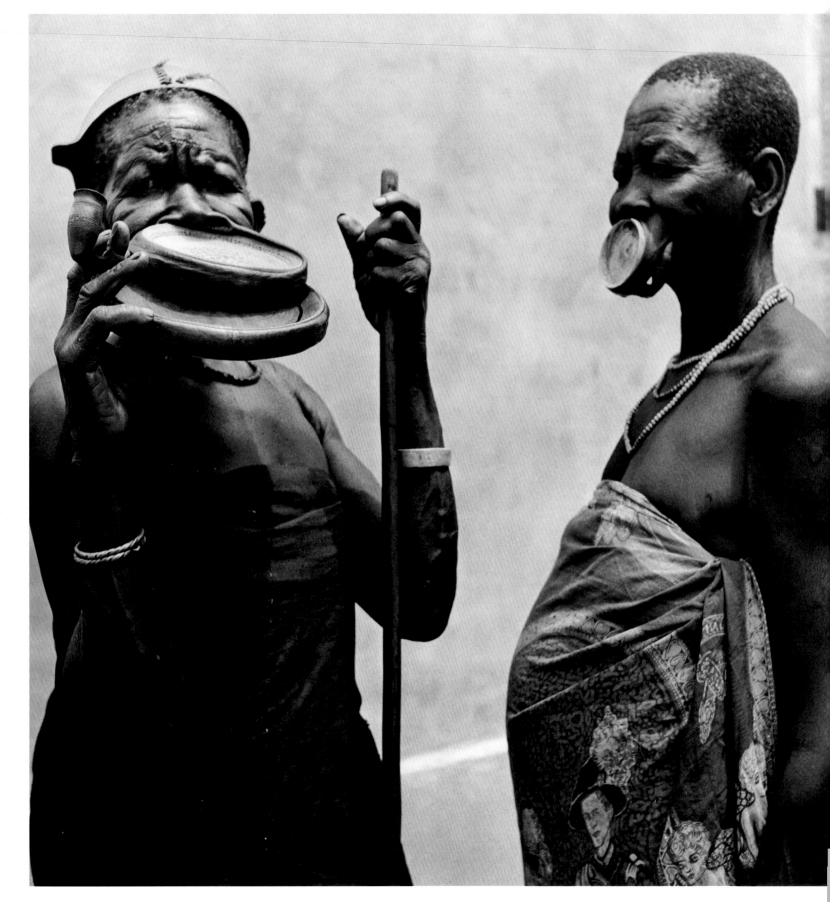

CHAD, AFRICA / 1952

""BEAUTIFUL YOUNG PEOPLE ARE ACCIDENTS

OF NATURE, BUT BEAUTIFUL OLD PEOPLE

ARE WORKS OF ART."

— ELEANOR ROOSEVELT

MATO GROSSO, BRAZIL / 1952

44

HUNGARY / 1935

CAIAPO WOMEN perform a ring dance, stamping their feet and chanting while moving in circles. They're arranged by social status: single, married without children, married with one child, married with more than one child. /above left

HUNGARIAN MAIDENS dressed in traditional costume perform a *karikazo*—a circle dance. The chain dance is symbolic of each individual's dependence on others for support, guidance, and direction. /above

LÓDZ, POLAND / 1987

MESCALARO INDIAN RESERVATION, NEW MEXICO / 1992

WEARING A GARLAND of white flowers—a symbol of innocence—a young Polish girl prays at her first communion. In Catholic Poland, first communion is an important step in life, celebrated by the entire community. /above left

PREPARING FOR THE SUNRISE CEREMONY, a young Apache girl stands quietly as her face is painted. Throughout the arduous four-day-long initiation as she enters womanhood, the community showers the girl with blessings. /above

IN LATVIA, A BRIDE on her way to church gives money to a beggar. It is a custom in many cultures for the bride and groom to give favors to others on their wedding day, to share their good fortune. /page 48

RIGA, LATVIA / 1990s

"WOMEN HAVE TO DO EVERYTHING A MAN DOES,

BUT BACKWARDS AND IN HIGH HEELS."

— GINGER ROGERS

XINJIANG, CHINA / 2004

IN XINJIANG, CHINA, song and dance are integral to an Uygur wedding. They impart messages of hope and goodwill to the new couple. Guests bring gifts of food. /above left

YOUNG PEOPLE DANCE the night away at a popular Blackpool, England, discotheque. Going out with friends is a common social pastime for the youth of most cultures. /below left

BLACKPOOL, ENGLAND / 1998

A GROUP OF WOMEN in Johannesburg, South Africa, celebrate their matriculation at a ball held in their honor. Such occasions reinforce the community bonds of friendship. /above right

A YOUNG WOMAN ROCKS to the beat at a concert in Salvador, Brazil. The collective energy of the people assembled intensifies their emotions, bonding them fleetingly. /below right

PRACTICING THE ANCIENT RITE of *ushi no koku mairi*, a Japanese woman nails a straw effigy to a shrine to curse the person who has wronged her—perhaps a cheating husband. /page 52

MEMBERS OF THE IRMANDADE da Nossa Senhora da Boa Morte, a religious society in the Candomblé faith, which blends Catholicism and African spiritualism, stand out by their manner of dress. /pages 54-55

JOHANNESBURG, SOUTH AFRICA / 1990s

SALVADOR, BRAZIL / 2002

"A Woman is like a teabag —

only in hot water do you realize

how strong she is."

— Nancy Reagan

CACHOEIRA, BRAZIL / 1992

Army of Roses
rooted in tradition

Martyrdom—sacrificing one's life for the sake of a principle or one's religious belief—is nothing new; there are countless saints of various religions who have suffered torture and death. Even so, such events took place hundreds of years ago and aren't modern concerns. In recent years, though, a shocking trend has emerged in nations around the world of more women seeking the path to martyrdom by becoming suicide bombers. So much so that certain tactics are taking on ritual proportions, complete with video recordings of their intentions. Why would women, the givers of life, choose to take life instead? During the United States' occupation of Iraq, hardly a day goes by without news of another suicide bombing. On the day that I write this, one American soldier and five Iraqis were killed in such an attack. These bombings have become disturbingly common tactics of war and have the power to penetrate the most formidable armies in the world. When a group of people feel outgunned and outmaneuvered by a more aggressive occupying force, taking one's own life in an effort to kill others has become strategy. For some Palestinians, Tamil Tigers, and Iraqis, martyrdom in the struggle for freedom or adherence to a cause has become the means of attaining hero status. For others, as the Chechen women suicide bombers—the so-called black widows—expressed it, it is an act to avenge husbands or other relatives killed in the decade-long war with Russia.

To look into these matters more closely, I visited a region all too familiar with suicide bombings: Israel and the

Occupied Territories. On January 27, 2002, Yassir Arafat, the late president of the Palestinian National Authority, had called for women to take up arms against the Israelis and fight for a free Palestine. He promised full equality between men and women. Women are not just "the womb of the nation," he said, "you are my 'Army of Roses' that will crush Israeli tanks."

In one explosive instant, a 26-year-old Palestinian woman answered his call. That very day, Wafa Idris became the first woman to blow herself up in a Jerusalem shoe store—killing one man and wounding more than a hundred other innocent people. She received a hero's funeral, attended by hundreds. Her picture was posted everywhere. Wafa was the first, but she would not be the last.

What motivated her? It was no secret that Wafa had been going through difficulties in her personal life. She was married, but unable to have children, and her husband divorced her. In addition, Wafa worked for the Red Crescent, a humanitarian aid organization that took care of the sick and wounded from the conflict. These personal issues, compounded by the bloodshed that she witnessed at work, could have made for a deadly combination. Not being able to give birth with its surrounding rituals, combined with the horrors of the country's occupation, may have led Wafa to act. In looking into the stories of women who had exploded themselves, patterns began to emerge that caused us to question the actual intent of some of the bombers. Did Wafa's inability to carry out one ritual lead her to take on another one? In Palestinian society, having children—and the rituals it involves—is not the right of a woman, but rather, her responsibility. She who cannot produce a child is sometimes deemed useless to society and a burden on one's family. When I asked her mother, whether Wafa would have killed herself had she been able to have children, her mother said, "No."

In quick succession, seven other women followed Wafa in the deadly rite. The youngest suicide bomber, Ayat Akhras, was only 18 years old, about to graduate from high school and engaged to be married. She had everything to live for, yet she chose death. Ayat exploded herself in a Jerusalem supermarket, killing two others and injuring 28.

The great irony of women taking steps to become suicide bombers is that, in Palestinian society, women were not always considered equal to men until Arafat's call to arms and his promise of equality. Barbara Victor, the author of *Army of Roses: Inside the World of Palestinian Suicide Bombers*, says that, until then, women were discouraged from participating in the resistance. "Islamic clerics were adamant that a woman's place was in the home with her family and not roaming the streets unchaperoned," she says. "The woman's proper function in life was to give birth as early and as often as possible."

The true intentions of the female suicide bombers may never be known because the only people with the answers are dead: the bombers themselves. Although this fateful step can easily be interpreted as a last resort for someone desperate, many suicide bombers come from educated, middle-class families with a future. Whatever their motivation, the ritual practices they are developing inspire other women to follow in their footsteps, taking their own, young lives and the lives of countless innocent people. For Wafa it was perhaps replacing a ritual of joy with death. For other women, going through the motions of a suicide bombing may mean martyrdom for the homeland. In their ritual, they prepare a statement or video of their intentions, have a photograph made for a hero's poster, strap on the explosives, and choose a highly populated target. Immediately upon their death, they are heralded as saviors, their photos plastered all over the land they've left.

In the struggle for equality, women have reached new positions the world over. Here the question remains whether the increasing presence of suicide bombing among women with its ritual overtones is a sign of the rising status of women in Muslim culture, or the frustrated expression of women's marginalization in that society.

—*Lisa Ling*

KABUL, AFGHANISTAN / 1993

JERUSALEM, ISRAEL / 1984

AN AFGHAN POSTER behind a girl exhorts Muslim women to cover themselves. To Westerners the burka symbolizes the oppression of women, but to many Muslim women the burka means modesty, purity, and righteousness. /above left

TO HONOR HER SON killed by an Israeli patrol, a grieving mother defiantly holds up a Palestinian flag, outlawed on the West Bank. By doing so, she shares her grief with the community and raises a national consciousness. /above

AN AFGHANI MUSLIM WOMAN under her proper burka invites comparison to the car under wraps in the foreground. Many societies around the world use clothing to denote their religious faith and/or ethnic affiliation. /pages 60-61

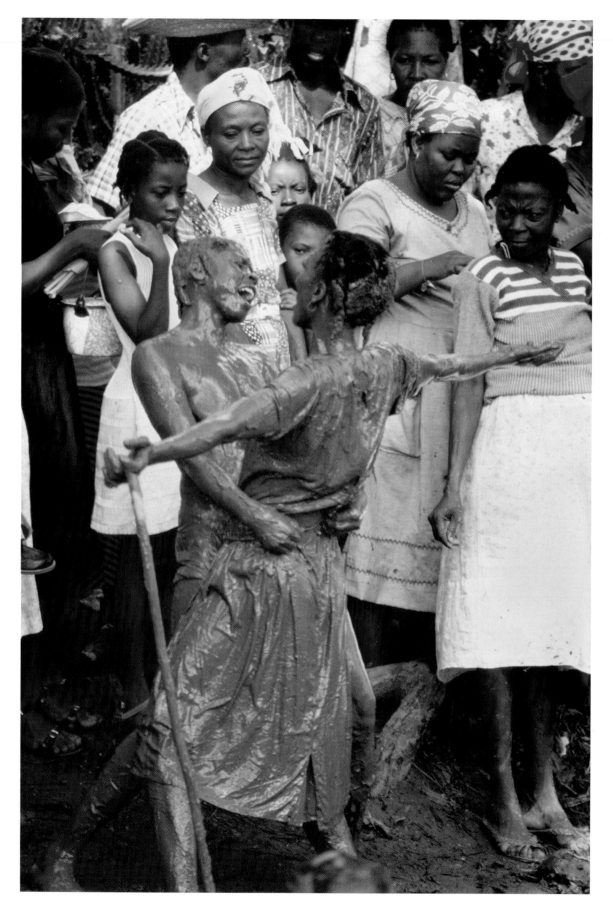

YOUNG WOMEN POSSESSED by the spirits dance on the edge of the sacred mud pond in Haiti at an annual voodoo festival honoring Ogou, the god of war, and Erzuli, the goddess of love. /left

IN A CASE OF VIRGIN WORSHIP, a *Kumari*—a prepubescent girl—the symbol of purity and the promise of fertility and prosperity, is carried through the streets of Patan, Nepal. /right

IN AN ARIAAL VILLAGE in Kenya, a newly circumcised bride rests with a friend inside a hut. Circumcision, the first part of the wedding ceremony, initiates the girl into womanhood. /page 65

LALITPUR, NEPAL / 1979

"WOMAN SOFTENS HER OWN TROUBLES

BY GENEROUSLY SOLACING THOSE OF OTHERS."

— FRANÇOISE D'AUBIGNE MAINTENON

MARSABIT DISTRICT, KENYA / 1999

MYANMAR / 1990s

66

KILAUEA, HAWAII / 2002

AN ELDERLY TIBETAN WOMAN spins a prayer wheel filled with mantras and prayers. The spinning connects the devotee's mind, body, and speech, and the supplications benefit all sentient beings. /above left

A YOUNG HAWAIIAN WOMAN plays a tune for Pélé, the mother goddess who has both destructive and creative powers of life. If Pélé accepts their offerings, worshipers believe that she "lends her strength and passions" to them. /above

MILAN, ITALY / 1992

FASHION MODELS PRIMP and prepare for the catwalk. In today's society the fashion model personifies the ultimate concept of beauty, influencing the body image of thousands of young women. /above

YOUNG HOPEFULS RELAX between practices for a model competition, hoping to be the next paradigm of beauty. Young girls frequently emulate fashion models, treating them as role models. /above right

NICE, FRANCE / 2000

A YOUNG WOMAN REJOICES at her high school graduation, the secular coming-of-age ritual in the United States. Family and friends gather to witness the ceremony, full of pomp and circumstance. /pages 70-71

THE WOMEN OF THE LATUKA TRIBE in Sudan wade into the muddy water to participate in an ancient fishing ritual. The ceremony endows the women with power and strengthens their community bonds. /page 72

SEVERAL YOUNG WOMEN line up to compete for the title of Potato Blossom Queen at a local festival in Maine. Beauty contests reinforce a community's perceptions of the ideal woman. /pages 74-75

TORIT, SUDAN / 1955

"MODESTY ANTEDATES CLOTHES

AND WILL BE RESUMED WHEN CLOTHES ARE

NO MORE. MODESTY DIED WHEN CLOTHES

WERE BORN. MODESTY DIED

WHEN FALSE MODESTY WAS BORN."

— MARK TWAIN

Family

Tasoulla Hadjiyanni, an architect and social scientist born in Cyprus, educated and teaching in the United States, was married in 1992 in Cyprus at her parents' home, where they hosted her wedding in the Greek Orthodox church tradition. For the ceremony she wore a white silk organza gown with a sheer veil covering her face, giving her an ethereal, dreamy quality.

As within Cypriot custom, the ritual began when the bride entered the formal living room to be "dressed" by her female friends and sisters. They arranged her hair in an upsweep, a common bridal fashion for the time, and did her makeup. After Tasoulla was properly attended to, her mother, followed by her father, came to her side to bless her by circling a small tray with two lighted candles three times above her head—a custom called "smoking" the bride. In addition to blessing her wedding, the ritual guarded her against the evil eye, should anyone have wished her bad luck.

Belief in the evil eye is not common to all religious beliefs, but it is found in several countries around the Mediterranean. The silver tray and candles, along with a perfume bottle filled with rosewater, are the usual gifts in Cyprus from the mother to the bride. Another ritual involves tying a red sash around the bride's waist, symbolizing a wish for fertility. This rite was omitted in the interest of shortening the ceremony. Tasoulla's wedding was a modern version of older, longer rituals. Younger people, who live in urban areas, have abandoned practices that included cooking for days to feed guests an elaborate meal and preparing a house for the newlyweds ("down to the last needle") to display to the guests.

An Egyptian woman proudly displays her child for all to see in a vintage photograph of 1911.

Musicians played typical Cypriot music with Cypriot instruments, which included one traditional song with sentimental verses that brought tears to everyone's eyes. Tasoulla translated the verses as follows:

Good times to you new bride,
Good times to you and hello,
Enjoy the angel [your husband]
Who will stand next to you.

Good times and golden times
And blessed times,
This job we have just started
To be well supported.
She changed and adorned herself
The white pigeon [the bride],
And she is going to church
With her own mate.

In the garden, your mother
Planted lavender
To cut and to smell
To always remember you.

Oh, my tender lemon tree
Down by the river
Shake and drop your blossoms
To fill the mattress [the bed of the newlyweds].

Call her mother
To come and "smoke" her [to take the evil eye away]
And to give her the blessing
To live a thousand years.

Call her father
To come and to put the belt around her,

[the red belt...]
And give her the wish
And give her away.

Although Tasoulla's marriage ceremony contained customs specific to the Greek Orthodox Church in Cyprus, the ritual was similar in many ways to formal marriage ceremonies elsewhere in the world. The bride's family bids her farewell at the wedding, as the ritual focuses on separating her from her relatives with the consequence of transferring primary allegiance to her husband, which in some cultures means allegiance to his family as well.

IF A MOTHER SENDS A SUBSTITUTE
FOR HER DAUGHTER DURING INITIATION,
HER DAUGHTER REMAINS A CHILD;
THE SUBSTITUTE BECOMES A WOMAN.

In Cyprus, however, this is not quite the case. As a dowry, the bride's parents build a house for her that is located near them, and she is expected to care for her parents, not her in-laws, in their old age. Thus, in Cyprus, families want to have daughters as well as sons. In addition, the bride's dowry gives her empowerment, for with a substantial dowry, she has a voice in decision-making, and she also owns her home in the case that the marriage is dissolved.

Wearing a veil over her face marks the bride's transition from separation to incorporation as she moves from being unmarried to being married. The parents bless their daughter's departure through the smoking ritual, and when the red belt is tied around the bride's waist, the parents express their best wishes for the bride's incorporation as a wife into a new family with her husband and as a potential mother.

Family rituals are more intimate than community events. Here, the definition of "family" must be understood: In many places around the world, "family" means the extended, biological family, not just the nuclear family of spouses and their offspring. Many rituals involve family members, either in initiating the ritual or carrying it through. Both fathers and mothers are important in setting up or sponsoring rituals for their daughters, especially in coming-of-age rituals when their daughters approach adulthood or marriage. Often mothers steep themselves in the separation rituals as their daughters prepare for the transition phase from being a bride to becoming a wife.

Among the Mende people in Sierra Leone, the mother, as a member of the Sande Society herself, takes responsibility for separating her daughter from being a child within the family by sending her daughter to the initiation encampment. A Mende proverb states, "Even if your mother sends a paid stand-in to take your place, nobody can [take your place]," because each girl must experience initiation firsthand. This rite gives girls access to custom and community. If a mother sends a substitute for her daughter, her daughter remains a child; the substitute, going through the transition of a Sande initiation, becomes a woman. Significantly, within the transition ritual—the Sande initiation—the daughter drops her childhood name to adopt a new one that indicates her incorporation into the fully adult, female world. Her mother, serving as her sponsor, acknowledges that the Sande initiation ritual simultaneously separates her from her family and her childhood and defines her as an adult, ready for marriage.

According to Mende expectations, after the completion of the initiation, the young woman, at age 15 or 16, immediately marries and soon after becomes pregnant. Although she lives with her husband's family after the wedding, she returns to the care of her mother when her delivery date draws near. The mother-daughter bond again becomes primary since it is understood that she is inexperienced. By staying with her mother, she is guided in learning to care for her baby, and maintains sexual abstinence from her husband for up to two years after the infant's birth. Custom decrees that she must not live with him at least until after the baby walks.

In Western cultures, universal patterns of initiation are not customary for girls, but similarities exist within different cultural traditions such as the quinceañera, a Spanish term for a girl's 15th birthday party; the sweet-sixteen party; the debutante ball; and the preparations for holding a wedding. In the case of the first three examples, families are deeply involved in most of the decision-making because resources from the family support the event. These celebrations also mark the end of childhood, as separation rituals, and introduce the daughter as a woman ready for marriage. Where there are two parents, both may contribute financial support, but mothers most often organize the party's details: the guest list, the menu, the decorations, and the selection of the daughter's gown. Sometimes mothers and daughters have different expectations about an appropriate dress in regard to its design, for example, how much décolletage and what color to choose. One mother with two daughters and two quinceañeras to plan wanted them to wear conservative styles. Her daughters wanted daring, revealing, "womanly" dresses.

Author Michele Salcedo in her guide to planning successful quinceañeras suggested a middle ground: a dress that appears grown-up but doesn't show too much skin.

Similarly Vendela Vida, who investigated initiation rites for girls and women throughout the United States, observed in her book *Girls on the Verge: Debutante Dips, Gang Drive-bys, and Other Initiations*, that mothers who have had their own quinceañera

"…are the ones with the dreams of their daughters' celebrations, and their daughters are born into these dreams. As one young woman [noted], "I wasn't even born yet and my mother was already saying 'I can't wait for her to have her fifteens.'"

The occasion of the quinceañeras was traditionally thought of as the launching of young women into the world of adulthood, allowing them the opportunity to go to parties, date young men, use cosmetics, wear high heels and more revealing clothing, and shave their legs. As times have changed, some observers believe that the parties have become either "just a party" or too ostentatious and have lost their significance as a mark for turning girls into women.

In a similar vein, debutante balls serve as rituals to launch daughters into society and indicate they are ready for marriage, according to Vida.

"…because they, the mothers, were debs, and their mothers before them were debs—many harbor a not-so-veiled hope that the ball will ensure their daughters will date and eventually marry someone of their own social class."

The most common expectation is that the ritual of participating in debutante balls allows the young women to make connections and to meet someone suitable for marriage. Many young women are also aware that as far as their parents are concerned, the young women have little choice in whether or not they make their debut. As one Houston debutante said:

"…My grandmother was a debutante, and so was my mother. My parents actually met at my mother's debutante ball—my father was someone else's escort. I've known since the day I was born that I was going to come out."

The sweet-sixteen parties appear removed from the coming-of-age initiations and debutante balls, rituals that ostensibly introduce one's daughter as an adult, ready for marriage. The sweet-sixteen message is that the girl is still on the brink of initiation. In the MTV series on sweet-sixteen parties, each program included the range of activities from initial planning through the execution. Primary among the activities was selecting the dress, a significant shopping occasion for mother and daughter, sometimes experienced as painless, and sometimes not. Mothers and daughters usually held long discussions about the right dress and often disagreed on what was age-appropriate. When mother and daughter shared similar values and had a strong bond, they quickly and easily selected the dress for the party, but not when friction existed between them. For example, in one episode, Ava and her mother disagreed during a shopping trip to Paris and returned home empty-handed when the mother decided that the dress her daughter wanted was not appropriate because she was "still a young girl." In fact, the daughter was in the process of separating from her family as a child, ready to be an adult, not already a sophisticated woman of the world. At home, where Ava had two dresses custom-made, she described her ideal dress as one that would be beige so that it would look as though she were "wearing nothing but rhinestones." She entered her Arabian

Nights-themed party by reclining on a rose-colored settee carried by four university polo players.

Such parties are expensive. Sierra, who proclaimed herself a "diva," celebrated a sweet-sixteen party at a cost of $200,000. The party was held a year early, when she was 15, because she wanted "to beat the crowd and have her bash one year early." She hired messengers, who were dressed in white and chauffeured in a limousine, to hand-deliver the invitations with a speech, along with a miniature pink Louis Vuitton cake. On her day, she entered the party two hours late, dressed in a flight jumpsuit as she arrived in a helicopter, and changed into

THE DAUGHTER WAS IN THE PROCESS OF SEPARATING FROM HER FAMILY AS A CHILD, READY TO BE AN ADULT, NOT ALREADY A SOPHISTICATED WOMAN.

five different outfits during the evening. Her parents' gift to her was a tiara, and in the fashion show presented as entertainment, Sierra starred as the model.

Coming-of-age parties, as rituals with a daughter having a mind of her own, stand in stark contrast to rituals for new babies. Although both parents are involved, mothers are instrumental in taking charge of the infant's care and in continuing that role for a significant period. Mothers—whether birth mother or mother through adoption—plan and carry out the ceremonies related to naming the baby, because entire families select and bestow the infant's name. Naming rituals emphasize the arrival and the incorporation of the newborn into the family. If the ritual for naming is carried out within a larger, public arena, the community affirms the family choice and acknowledges the arrival of the child. Often, the baby's name, as provided by either or both parents, is recorded officially on a birth certificate at the hospital in fulfillment of government requirements, an act that does not serve as a ritual in itself. The name is bestowed ritually through a special ceremony for naming, or christening, an infant.

The family's role in a baby's naming ritual normally involves the mother choosing and supplying the garments needed, even if she is not an active participant. Often special requirements for clothing are stipulated, as in the Greek Orthodox baptism, for which everything from underwear, socks, and outer garments must be completely new. In that case, the godparents purchase a set of white clothes for the baby to wear after its baptism in the church in "a naked state." The priest immerses the infant in water, then anoints it with olive oil and wraps it in a new linen cloth for the next portion of the ritual, called the Chrismation (confirmation). The baby is dressed in the new garments, and the priest says, "Clothed is the servant of God (give name) with the garment of righteousness, in the Name of the Father, and of the Son, and of the Holy Spirit. Amen," indicating that the child begins an entirely new life.

Following this ceremony, four locks of hair are cut from the infant's head and shaped into a cross. Hair represents strength; an offering of hair serves as a promise "for the child to serve God with all its strength." Members of the entire family are involved. A firstborn male child should be named after the husband's father, so that the grandfather's full name will continue. A firstborn female child is often named after the maternal grandmother. The many-phased ritual takes the infant through a transition culminating in incorporation as a full-fledged member of the church. On completion of the ritual, the godparents present the newly dressed baby to the mother.

Rachida Chida and Zina Chida, sisters-in-law living in Tunisia, North Africa, describe the family rituals surrounding a new mother as follows: A young woman is still considered a bride until her first child is born. Her mother makes sure that the proper rituals for her daughter and grandchild are carried out. Part of her daughter's trousseau includes special clothes kept for her to wear after she delivers her firstborn child, whether a boy or a girl. She helps pack her daughter's suitcase for the hospital with new clothes for the baby and dressy pajamas for the mother-to-be so that her daughter will "look her best" when family and friends stream to her room with flowers and gifts. Often she decorates her daughter's hands and feet with henna before she leaves for the hospital. As a new grandmother, she oversees a successful celebration after the arrival of a healthy newborn. She prepares a special, sweet delicacy, called *zrir,* to serve the guests, made by finely grinding roasted almonds, hazelnuts, sesame seeds, mixed with honey and butter. The more finely ground, the more delicate is the treat. The sweet is served warm in special glasses with a spoon. The use of expensive, imported nuts demonstrates the epitome of family hospitality, so that, at times, zrir is made wholly of pistachios, which are the most expensive nuts.

At home, the new mother is required to have bed rest; her mother may stay with her for a week or arrive daily to care for her until the husband returns from work. Typically, she prepares dishes such as vegetable soup, grilled beef, and kidneys for her daughter and also serves as hostess to greet guests as they arrive. When the child is seven days old, the baby has its first bath—in contrast to gentle cleansing—in the midst of a party. The new mother wears a traditional dress such as an embroidered robe, called a *jebba,* and the baby wears a robe made of lace. Dinner is served, and sometimes families in cities, such as El Kef, west of the capital, sacrifice a sheep to cook with couscous to serve the guests.

During the next few weeks, many family members play a part—a sister, cousin, or aunt may alternate with the mother to help care for her daughter, teaching her how to raise a baby for the first time.

When the baby is 40 days old, another celebration is held for the mother, viewed as "second wedding," starting with a visit to the Turkish bath. This ritual is said to

WHEN THE BABY IS 40 DAYS OLD, ANOTHER CELEBRATION IS HELD FOR THE MOTHER, VIEWED AS A SECOND WEDDING, STARTING WITH A VISIT TO THE TURKISH BATH.

celebrate the young woman's return to life as wife and sexual partner, marking the end of her transition into motherhood. The party can be as elaborate as finances allow with family members, perhaps cousins and aunts, helping to put on as big a party as affordable. The bigger, the better.

Still another ritual, the *karkoush,* celebrates the appearance of the baby's first front teeth, usually by the age of six months. Family members, friends, and their children bring parcels of mixed nuts, candy, and roasted wheat kernels to the festivity. The baby sits in the middle of a new sheet of fine linen or a cloth embellished with embroidery placed on the floor, and the goodies are slowly poured over its head. As the guests make joyful sounds of ululation, the children gather around, jostling each other in an effort to catch the candy and nuts, adding to the fun as everyone watches the baby cry, giggle, or laugh.

These Tunisian rituals emphasize the incorporation of both baby and mother as they enter the next stage of life. For the mother, the rituals stress being identified as "mother," and for the baby, the rituals stress entering the next stage of growth and development.

At both the beginning and the end of life, families are important. This is true for participation of the extended family at funerals, as well as their involvement during the first year of birth.

Among the Kalabari of Nigeria, extended family members set up and carry out an elaborate funeral celebration to honor the life of an elder at the time of death, whether grandmother, grandfather, mother, father, aunt, or uncle. The elder's offspring must organize and support the costs involved to celebrate the successful life of their deceased relative. The spouse remains completely apart from the funeral activities, and does not attend the rituals, except to show up once, to sing a song, and then must be secluded to mourn privately.

The body of a deceased elder is kept frozen or embalmed to allow enough time for the extended members of the family to meet and plan the elaborate funeral, including a financial pledge to underwrite the expenses. After the date is set and plans are completed, the relatives bring the corpse from the mortuary to the family home where the body is laid out on a bed of state. The chief mourners—the eldest son or daughter and their siblings—along with the brothers and sisters of the deceased and any grandchildren or grandnieces and grandnephews dress in specified wrappers and blouses, if women, and elegant robes, if men. They pay respect to their loved one and move the corpse from bed to bed in the home within a 24-hour period before burial. After the burial, the relatives host the remainder of the funeral celebration for the townspeople, which lasts for another week. Women relatives play a prominent role in decorating the funeral beds with textiles loaned from the extended family "cloth boxes." During the week between the day of burial and the last two nights, women practice their dancing and also guard the decorated beds. For the final day parade by the extended family through the town, both men and women dress in specific garments, and then change to another prescribed set of outfits for the final night. A highlight of the parade is the number of female relatives dressed appropriately in traditional madras wrappers that are a signature fabric for the Kalabari people. In the evening, embroidered velvet garments and striped silks are preferred. A Christian family arranges a thanksgiving prayer at Sunday services following the final funeral night; family members dress up and walk to church from their family compound and sit together at the front of the church.

The various aspects of the Kalabari funeral ritual stress the separation of the deceased from life. Family members bid farewell on the last night when they complete a final dance, ending with a special drum beat; then they line up and leave the compound, dispersing quickly into the night. They have sent the deceased member off to join their ancestors by emphasizing family success in their ability to stage an impressive performance for his or her departure.

Rituals, such as coming-of-age ceremonies or those marking birth and death, highlight the special connections between mothers and daughters, and between women and their families around the world. Each ritual can be analyzed for emphasizing departure, transition, or incorporation, for it exists in infinite variety, depending on the specific cultural context in which it is found.

"THE BITTEREST TEARS SHED OVER GRAVES

ARE FOR WORDS LEFT UNSAID AND

DEEDS LEFT UNDONE."

— HARRIET BEECHER STOWE

TUTUILA, AMERICAN SAMOA / 2000

A MOTHER IN HAVANA, CUBA, performs a spiritism ritual to cleanse her daughter of evil spirits. Cigar smoke draws out evil, while the intoned prayers protect the girl against future trouble, in a blend of African and Catholic rites. /pages 84-85

A BOSNIAN WOMAN IN SERBIA grieves for her children. On the anniversary of the massacre at Srebrenica, where Serbs killed thousands of her countrymen, a woman remarked of Serb women, "We are all mothers." /pages 86-87

GALILEE REGION, ISRAEL / 1995

JOYFUL, YET SAD, a Samoan mother helps her daughter dress in one of two wedding gowns, one to wear to the service and one to the reception, as of old, although Western-style customs now prevail in Samoa. /above left

OVERCOME BY EMOTION, a Palestinian bride sheds tears of joy for her upcoming nuptials. Female friends and family perform the bride's ritualized preparation amid much giggling and gossiping. /above

IN MACEDONIA, the extended family celebrates a boy's circumcision with a three-day extravaganza of food, song, and dance. Here, they dance counterclockwise around the young initiate, cradled in his mother's arms. /pages 90-91

89

Mothers without Borders

rooted in tradition

THE TRADITIONAL PRACTICES OF BECOMING A NEW MOTHER — CHILDBIRTH CLASSES, PARENTING CLASSES, AND THE BONDING THAT GOES WITH A CONGENIAL GROUP OF WOMEN GOING THROUGH THE PROCESS TOGETHER — HAVE FOR MANY WOMEN BEEN REPLACED BY ADOPTION RITUALS. ACROSS THE UNITED States some 22,000 foreign children are adopted each year. Of the circumstances I have witnessed, adoptions of Chinese girls by Americans are joyous occasions.

The availability of girls for adoption goes back to China's Cultural Revolution, when Communist Party Chairman Mao Zedong encouraged his people to give birth to more Communist Party members. His words spurred a population explosion, the likes of which the world had never seen. By 1979, unable to control this mass of humanity and provide for all of its people, the Chinese government began limiting the number of children couples could have to one. This rule became known as the "One Child Policy." But the policy had consequences that China's leadership did not anticipate. China's society has traditionally placed more value on boys than on girls, because boys carry on the family name. Although during China's Communist years, Mao Zedong declared boys and girls equal with his famous saying, "Girls hold up half the sky," things changed when couples were restricted to having only one child. Particularly in the countryside, if a couple can have only one child, boys are seen as having a greater economic benefit to the family. A girl will inevitably marry and be enveloped into the husband's family, leaving her own parents to work the fields and grow old alone. A boy, on the other hand, will marry and bring his new wife into his family home, adding more bodies—assuming they have children—to the household to work. "A son will take care of us," a country woman in China's Anhui province told me. "A daughter will just leave."

As a consequence, thousands of baby girls have been aborted, abandoned, or killed over the last decade. So many women were aborting upon learning the fetus was female that the government banned the use of ultrasound to determine gender. The impact of the government's one child policy is being felt throughout the countryside, particularly in primary schools. I visited a school in the Guangdong province, where the average number of children per classroom was 35; 28 of whom were boys. The gender imbalance is growing so rapidly that by the year 2020, there will be about 20 million more men than women. The ramifications of such a disproportionate population may be felt all over the region. Experts say that China could become a society prone to increased violence and bullying; and women could be in danger of higher levels of abuse. There have already been cases of women being kidnapped from poor villages and sold to men in other parts of the country as wives. The Chinese government has acknowledged the potential problems the disparity may bring. Public education campaigns have been implemented to stop the abandonment of baby girls. Signs blanket China's countryside with such slogans as, "Respect Girls," and "Boys and Girls are Equal."

Baby girls who are abandoned face uncertain futures. They are found in parks, and on the steps of hospitals, police stations, or orphanages, often with notes asking that the baby girl be brought to safety and nurtured. I met Ye Ching, a shop owner in the Anhui Province, who had a son, but whose two sisters had given up baby girls. One sister was lucky enough to have a boy on the second try. After giving birth to three girls, Ms. Ye's other sister was still trying to have a son. She told me that giving up their baby girls was painful for her sisters. "Women are under so much pressure to have boys to carry on the family name," said Ms. Ye. "We have to have boys."

Out of this tragedy comes the joy of adoptive parenthood for many childless Americans. While most of the abandoned girls will remain in orphanages until adulthood, the lucky ones end up in places like Birmingham, Alabama; Atlanta, Georgia; and Houston, Texas. The majority of foreign-born adoptees come to the United States from China. Last year alone, an estimated 7,000 Chinese girls became U.S. citizens. Recently I accompanied 20 American couples to China; some were adopting their second Chinese baby. What I found amazing was that some of these couples had never traveled outside their home state. One woman had never before flown on an airplane. Yet, they all traveled to a distant land for a new ritual, to adopt a little girl who would change their life. The day these couples got their babies was a highly emotional one. Denise Hall from Atlanta proclaimed, "not far away there's a little girl who has never known a mother, or a father, or a sister. Today she's going to get all of those things."

After committing to adoption, the parents had to go through long rituals: filling out papers, enduring uncertain waiting periods, underwriting serious expenses, taking a long journey to a foreign country, and acquainting themselves with a different culture. In China, they found they were among peers with similar concerns. As new parents most of them now subscribe to the family network of adoptive parents for continued support, and many embrace a blending of cultures in rearing these children.

I was struck by what little ambassadors these girls have become. They have been catalysts for many Americans who have sought to acquaint themselves with Chinese culture. These little people help bridge a cultural gap between two countries that have historically had a contentious relationship. They will inevitably have opportunities to pursue the highest levels of education, and I believe that some of them may go back and change China.

—*Lisa Ling*

MONGOLIA / 1996

"GOD COULD NOT BE EVERYWHERE,

AND THEREFORE HE MADE MOTHERS."

— JEWISH PROVERB

JALISCO STATE, MEXICO / 1997

NILGIRI HILLS, INDIA / 1967

MOTHERS THE WORLD OVER delight in inhaling their baby's scent. Scent is one of the important bonding mechanisms between a mother and child, and it stimulates the child's developing senses. /page 94

THANKS TO THE PAINTED peyote cactus marks on her face and a shaman's incantations, a Huichol girl can make an imaginary journey of gathering peyote with her elders. /above left

TWO YOUNG TODA WOMEN, each pregnant with her first child, participate in a pre-birth ritual, requiring them to stare unblinkingly at a flame until it burns out. /below left

A 15-YEAR-OLD GIRL PRIMPS for her *quinceañera,* a religious ceremony and social announcement of her entrance into womanhood. The family proudly presents the new woman at an elaborate celebration. /above right

IN TRINIDAD, A MOTHER helps a young Hindu bride with her veil. In Hindu tradition, the bride wears red, the color of happiness, and the ceremony is held at the home of the bride's parents. /below right

WEARING THE TRADITIONAL white dress that signifies her innocence, a debutante enjoys the social whirl of the coming-out ball that marks her transition from child to adult. /page 98

CONFUSED AND UPSET, a child bride of the Rabari people of Rajasthan, India, is taken to visit her new in-laws. Her equally young husband stands beside her. The bride then returns to her parents' home until she reaches adulthood. /pages 100-101

FALLS CHURCH, VIRGINIA / 2001

CHARLOTTEVILLE, TRINIDAD AND TOBAGO / 1994

GREENWICH, CONNECTICUT / 1990s

"Being a princess isn't

all it's cracked up to be."

—Princess Diana

A POKOT WOMAN of Kenya bathes her child with squirts of water. The Pokot relieve a mother of duties during the postpartum period so she can devote time and energy to the child. /left

A **Maltese grandmother's** warm embrace speaks of strong family traditions. Grandmothers the world over form special bonds with their grandchildren. /right

At a maternity ward in Tiranë, Albania, a young mother smiles with pride and contentment at her newborn child. /page 105

"Giving birth is little more than a set

of muscular contractions granting passage

of a child. Then the mother is born."

— Erma Bombeck

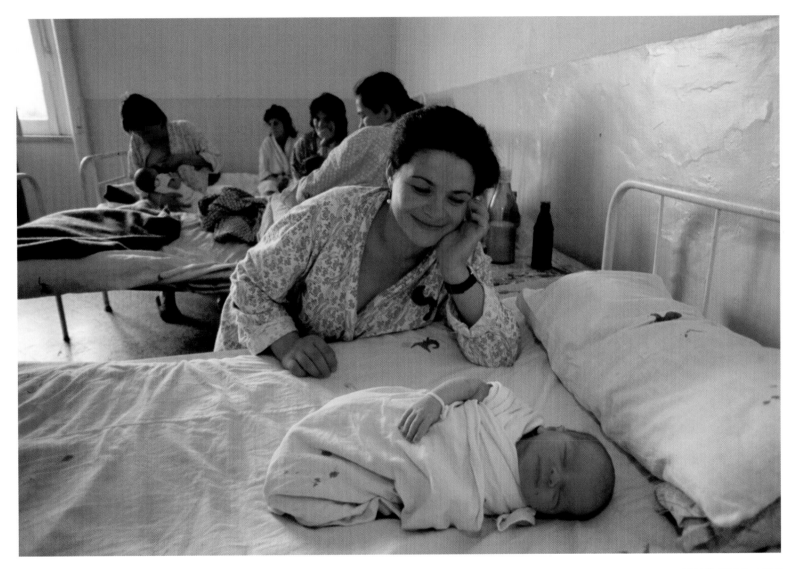

TIRANË, ALBANIA / 1992

SALT LAKE CITY, UTAH / 1996

TIBET, CHINA / 1999

A POLYGYMOUS FUNDAMENTALIST Mormon family—the husband surrounded by four wives—sits for its portrait. This Mormon group believes that "plural marriage is essential to achieving the highest degree of heaven." /above left

A POLYANDROUS FAMILY — a woman married to two brothers—in Tibet, represents a choice, not a tradition. This form of marriage does not fragment the family or the land, enabling a higher standard of living for all. /above

SILVER ORNAMENTS ADORN a young Tibetan mother's hair. She will pass on the baubles to her daughter and teach her to value them. Women rarely cut their hair; they use it to display their finery and wealth. /pages 108-109

ANTÉCUMA PATA, FRENCH GUIANA / 1983

KIMBERLEY, AUSTRALIA / 1992

AMONG THE WAYANA INDIANS of French Guiana, initiation rites at puberty for girls and boys involve a kunana—a wicker shield embedded with large black ants. The initiates must endure the painful stings without complaint. /above left

AN ABORIGINE GRANDMOTHER and great-grand-mother in Australia perform a smoking ceremony on the newest member of the family. They strongly believe in the healing properties of smoke to purify, bless, and protect her. /above right

A HAWAIIAN MOTHER and child lovingly touch foreheads and noses in a traditional Hawaiian *honi*. In this ancient greeting, the two inhale at the same time, exchanging *Ha* (the breath of life) and *mana* (spiritual power). /pages 112-113

KUAUI, HAWAII / 1998

The Dowry Debt *rooted in tradition*

OPEN ANY NEWSPAPER IN INDIA, AND YOU WILL FIND COUNTLESS ADVERTISEMENTS FROM PARENTS SEEKING MARRIAGEABLE PARTNERS FOR THEIR CHILDREN. THOUGH THINGS ARE CHANGING, A GREAT MANY MARRIAGES IN INDIA ARE STILL ARRANGED. THE PRESSURE FOR PARENTS TO MARRY OFF THEIR DAUGHTERS IS immense, because once a woman passes a certain age, the possibility of her marrying becomes greatly reduced.

Women are often seen as financial burdens. If a woman does not marry, she continues to put a strain on the family's resources, as one more mouth to feed. At the time of marriage, there is the ritual and unwritten obligation for the parents of the bride to pay a dowry to the family of their future son-in-law. Demanding dowry is illegal in today's India. According to the Dowry Prohibition Act of 1961, the punishment for giving or taking dowry is a fine and a prison term of no less than five years. The law, however, excludes presents given either to the bride or the groom. Dowry comes in many forms: cash, cars, appliances, and electronics. The husband's family will be the one taking on an additional person, and the dowry is meant as insurance for the daughter's proper treatment. A dowry is not limited to any particular class. Often, the more educated the groom, the higher the dowry that is expected. The man's parents have paid much to educate their son, so his future wife's family should pay more for the honor. India is not the only culture where paying dowry is an age-old ritual. In India, however, dowry demands have become so severe that it has taken on deadly consequences for some families who are unable to meet such demands.

Hardly a day goes by when the pages of India's newspapers do not contain stories of dowry-related abuses. Even in India's most technologically advanced city of Bangalore, there are more reports of deaths due to the inability to fulfill dowry demands than due to traffic accidents. Brides with insufficient funds may be starved, beaten, or shot to death. But the most horrific and, shockingly, the most common method is known as "bride burning." A woman's arms are held together as her husband or members of his family douse her with kerosene and set her ablaze. Those who survive are so badly maimed that they are further shunned by society, and labeled as failing in their marriage. The woman's hopes of ever marrying again are dashed, and she will be forced to move back in with her family (if they take her), where she will once again become a burden.

Although abuse of women is a serious problem worldwide, I was in utter disbelief that a society could treat a woman so cruelly until I witnessed the effects firsthand. I met Uma, a woman who was nearly burned to death five years ago. Her husband had been pressuring her to get more money from her family. After repeatedly proclaiming her inability to pay, he barged into her room one night and set her on fire. In an attempt to save her mother, their four-year-old daughter ran into the room and jumped onto her mother. Both mother and daughter survived, but with third degree burns over their faces and bodies. When I met them two years later, I was dismayed by how embarrassed the six-year-old child was about her appearance. Only when her mother asked her would Asha raise her little head. Uma told me that Asha is often harassed by her classmates. One day after she picked up Asha from school, I followed them to Uma's family home. When we arrived, her mother screamed at Uma for bringing a television crew along. "Already you bring us shame by being here; now everyone will know what happened." Rather than helping Uma bring her story to the world, her own family condemned her for bringing them unnecessary attention.

Women's organizations point to the seriousness of the situation. According to the Ahmedabad Women's Action Group, in Gujarat state, research shows that a thousand women are burned alive annually in that state alone. Often, those found culpable are a man's mother and his sisters. It's not uncommon to encounter entire families in prison for the crime of harming or killing a daughter-in-law. In New Delhi's Tihar Prison, the largest one in India, the majority of women are there for the murder of a male family member's wife. One section of the prison is unofficially known as the "mother-in-law wing." These crimes are happening with such frequency that an organization, the International Society Against Dowry Abuse and Bride Burning in India (ISADABBI), was created in 1993 to prevent the dowry practice and its consequences.

One might think that the public awareness campaign would reduce the number of cases, or that India's recent economic prosperity would decrease the pressure on families to pay. But, as Donna Fernandez of the Vimochina Women's Organization said, "the economic changes have not made things better; they've made people greedier."

Fernandez took me to the biggest hospital in Bangalore. The entire floor—more than 50 beds—was devoted to female burn victims, almost all of whom were dowry cases. In my years of reporting, I had never experienced such a heart-wrenching scene. As soon as I walked onto the floor, I heard the moans. I couldn't escape the smell of burning flesh. Bed after bed held charred bodies. Some cried in anguish, others lay there barely breathing. My nurse escort told me that when they are first admitted, almost all of them say that they incurred such wounds by "stove burst." A guard stands watch 24 hours a day to ensure that husbands or in-laws don't come back to finish the job. After a couple of days, when they know they are safe, many women admit that they were attacked.

Months after returning to America, I called Fernandez to check on several of the women. She told me that every single woman who was there during my visit had died.

—Lisa Ling

ANDHRA PRADESH, INDIA / 1994

"I DON'T THINK THERE HAS EVER BEEN A MAN,

WHO TREATED A WOMAN AS AN EQUAL,

AND THAT'S ALL I WOULD HAVE ASKED,

FOR I KNOW I'M WORTH AS MUCH AS THEY."

— BERTHE MORISOT

KWAZULU-NATAL PROVINCE, SOUTH AFRICA / 2000

THE BANJARA, A NOMADIC PEOPLE of India,
invest their wealth in silver jewelry and clothing
inset with mirrors—part of their dowry. The women
wear the ensemble each day, no matter how
impractical it may be on occasion. /page 116

A 17-YEAR-OLD ZULU WOMAN dances at her
umemulo—her coming-of-age ceremony. The
extended family celebrates her symbolic passing
from childhood to adulthood with song and dance
and pins money on her for good fortune. /above

GALLIANO, LOUISIANA / 1990

AT A CAJUN WEDDING, family and friends pin money to the bride to "pay" for the honor of dancing with either the bride or groom. The tradition, of European origin, ensures that the couple starts life together in good standing. /above

IN AMERICAN SAMOA, a mother and a fellow parishioner amuse a young child during the service. Worshipping together plays a strong role in the development of family and community bonds in many cultures. /pages 120-121

HOLDING HER BABY CLOSE, a Pisac Indian of Peru places a kiss on the child's cheek. Mothers around the world demonstrate affection in many different ways, but this pose is nearly universal. /pages 122-123

TUTUILA, AMERICAN SAMOA / 2000

"WOMEN, WHO ARE BEYOND

ALL DOUBT, THE MOTHERS OF ALL MISCHIEF,

ALSO NURSE THAT BABE TO SLEEP

WHEN HE IS TOO NOISY."

— RICHARD DODDRIDGE BLACKMORE

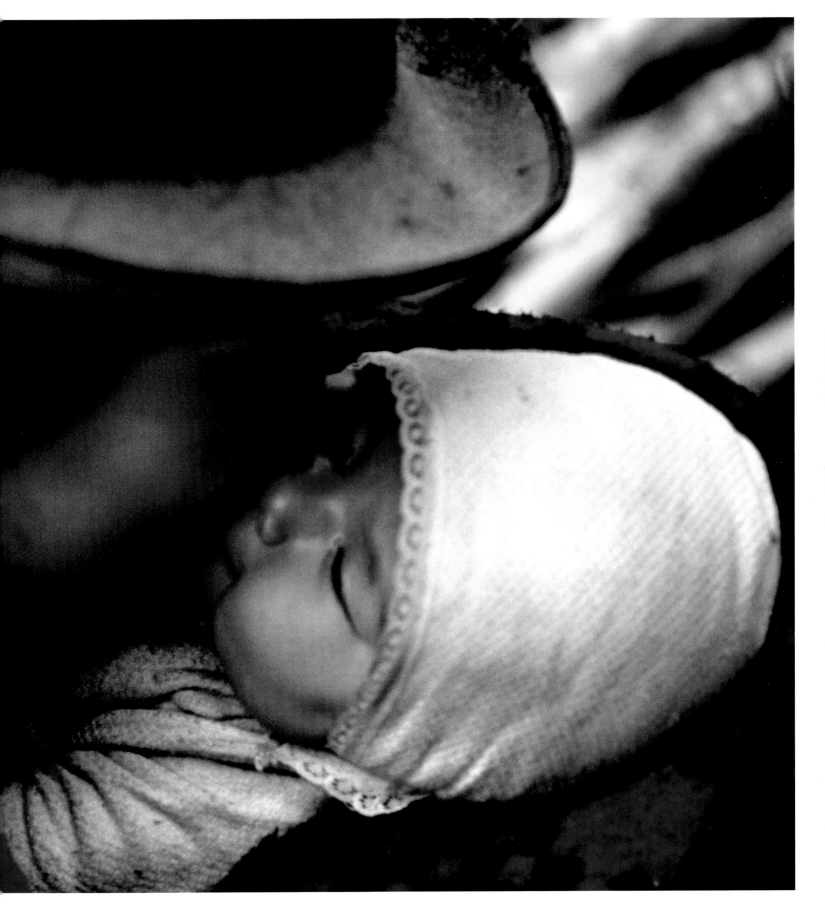

PISAC, PERU / 1996

Sisterhood

WHEN I AM AN OLD WOMAN, I SHALL WEAR PURPLE, WITH A RED HAT WHICH DOESN'T GO, AND DOESN'T SUIT ME…" (JENNY JOSEPH). RED HATS AND PURPLE DRESSES ARE BADGES OF THE RED HAT SOCIETY. IN 1998, SUE ELLEN COOPER SPIED A RED HAT IN A THRIFT SHOP AND REMEMBERED THE POEM

to justify buying the hat. "There it was. Such a beautiful, brilliant color! Such a jaunty devil-may-care attitude! Such a serendipitous find!… Before I knew it, that bright red fedora was perched on my head, dipping daringly below one eyebrow," she wrote later. Spurred on by her purchase, she bought others as birthday gifts for her friends age 50 and older as a joke and as a way to face the challenge of aging. Soon she and her friends with red hats also found purple dresses, and decided to wear their unusual outfits to a tea party at a local tearoom. Amused and buoyed by the fun of the event, Sue Ellen launched the Red Hat Society and declared herself Founder and Queen Mother.

Thus begins a tale of a modern-day ritual of sisterhood. By wearing red hats and purple dresses, these women, who numbered a million members in 35,000 chapters as of February 2005, acknowledge the fact of aging, and have fun in doing so. The ritualized act of wearing a specific color hat and dress allows them as a group, by developing a sisterhood, to admit that they are leaving youth behind and are making the transition to becoming older, while keeping a lively perspective. They flaunt their playfulness in the face of prejudices associated with aging, a transition not easy to make for women growing old in Western societies that value youth. Yet the idea behind the Red Hat Society has attracted so many

Genetics bind these two young sisters in a relationship that will last a lifetime.

followers that the group holds annual conventions and issues a publication, *The Red Hat Society LifeStyle Magazine*.

The Red Hat Society is only one example of ritualizing sisterhood, but sisterhood as an idea has many facets. Biological sisterhood involves commitments to each other as a family, with family rituals and ties that unite the sister (and sometimes split them if rivalry emerges). Social sisterhood, as in the case of Catholic sisterhood (sometimes called Women Religious), involves commitments of women to each other as belonging to groups that not only emphasize being female, but also are restricted to females. Nonbiological sisterhood rituals exist across cultures.

In Morocco, in the following example, sisterhood rituals are especially important in preparing a bride. As Fatima, an Amazigh (Berber) bride, waits patiently to have her hands and feet hennaed, one special friend known as a *wazira* is assigned to act as official witness that the bride's appropriate prenuptial activities take place, including dressing the bride. Other women, both relatives and friends, attend to her makeup, garments, and accessories, as described by Tiziana and Gianni Baldizzone in *Wedding Ceremonies: Ethnic Symbols, Costumes, and Rituals:*

"…One woman busies herself with a vase containing an oil for making Fatima's hair shine; an essential element in Berber eroticism. Meanwhile, another woman brings up a flask of rosewater, a third fetches a *serwal,* the cotton pantaloons gathered tight at the knee, while yet another carries in the white muslin bridal chemise, then a brooch, a silver pin and a ring. There is also a necklace made of cloves for its beneficial properties.

…Her female relations and friends vie with one another to lend Fatima a piece of jewelry, since the common Berber belief is that, by the time it is returned, a little of the good luck, her *baraka,* has rubbed off on it. The room set aside for her wedding preparations is restricted to only women, the bride and those attending her. The support of women around the bride is critical to the success for the bride's preparation for the ceremony."

In anthropologist Arnold van Gennep's analysis of ritual, this room exemplifies the idea of a physical place that allows the transition to occur between the separation from her family and the incorporation into her new family. The women who help prepare her dress know that certain items are not only appropriate, but will also bring her good fortune as a bride, in which they want to

CHANGES HAVE TAKEN PLACE RECENTLY, FOR WEDDING SHOWERS ARE NOW OFTEN GIVEN FOR THE BRIDAL COUPLE, WITH BOTH MALE AND FEMALE FRIENDS INCLUDED.

share. Her borrowed silver bracelets, for example, include specifically those decorated with 12 prongs, indicating strength among Imazighen (Berber) women. The circular shape of the bracelets symbolizes females, and silver, known as the metal of the moon, protects the bride from bad luck when she wears the bracelets.

Brides around the world have sisterhood support of various types relating to wedding rituals. In the United States, bridal showers given by the fiancee's closest friend or friends traditionally had a guest list of only women, and the bridesmaids for a formal wedding were always included. Some changes have taken place recently, for wedding showers are now often given for the bridal couple, with both male and female friends included.

In another development, bachelorette parties have been created, organized by the bride's female friends, usually her bridesmaids, and the parties often feature a male stripper, naughty party games, and bawdy jokes. The events parallel the raucous bachelor parties that were once reserved for the groom and his friends for a last night out before the wedding. These parties mark the departure of being single.

Coming-of-age activities, as socioculturally defined (because physical and sociocultural maturation are not always parallel), also produce the feeling of sisterhood, particularly because the rituals attached provide an opportunity for bonding among the participants. For example, among the Mende people of Sierra Leone, families separate their daughters at initiation age and seclude them from the community in an area called *kpanguima*. This kpanguima is an encampment, where the girls live to learn how to become a Sande Society member through a series of rituals. The Sande Society is significant because it acts as a powerful patron of the arts by commissioning masks that are worn by women for ceremonial dances.

Anthropologist Sylvia Boone, who conducted research on the Sande Society in the 1970s, reported, "It is the only known instance in Africa in which women customarily wear [carved, wooden] masks," a fact that for many years was ignored or unknown as a part of West African art and culture.

Without participation in Sande ritual, a female remains a child in Mende society, never attaining adulthood. The area of encampment for initiates and for already initiated women is off-limits to men, children, or anyone else not a member. Within the encampment, initiates are taught how to be a Sande woman in what is known as the Sande School, where they learn how to be acceptable wives, mothers, and community members in

Mende terms. An important skill learned during the initiation is how to dance, often under the tutelage of a tough dance mistress. Before entering the encampment, the girls are considered to be mere children, but after completing the initiation requirements, they return to the community, acknowledged as women. If a mother refuses to allow her daughter to be initiated, her daughter is never considered to be a woman, even though her body has matured physically.

Life as an initiate, living and interacting with other women, helps a young woman train to be a junior wife, because her life as a wife will be spent, not with her husband, but with her co-wives and many other female family members.

In the encampment, a bond of sisterhood becomes easily established. Attitude toward and availability of food changes because the women abandon the usual protocol for eating in the home, where women serve their husbands first and eat after the men finish. Here a junior wife does not need permission from a senior wife to "dip into the pot," and friends meet and eat together without having to be cautious about what they say in front of their household seniors. During the Sande encampment, cooking lessons are part of the initiates' curriculum, and those already initiated come back for "advanced courses" in cooking and healing practices. Opportunities for rituals related to sisterhood abound for Mende women. Sharing, generosity, and friendship are encouraged during—and result from—the rituals of Sande initiation and yearly renewal.

In the United States, strong friendships among girls and women develop from participating in situations strikingly different from those experienced by Mende girls and women. Nevertheless, American women have many opportunities for developing bonds of sisterhood with ritual behavior. A common example arises when a group of girls band together to participate in activities both during and after school. These friendship groups frequently continue after graduation day, emerging into strong sisterhoods with long-lasting bonds. Fictional sisterhoods exist in a variety of media, such as Robert Harling's *Steel Magnolias,* the play and subsequent movie of the same name; *Angry Housewives Eating Bonbons,* a novel by Lorna Landvik; and *Divine Secrets of the Ya-Ya Sisterhood* by Rebecca Wells, a novel made into a movie. But plenty of real life examples exist.

In 1980, as members in a women's professional group, four of us spun off to meet for lunch throughout each year, and we have done so on a regular basis for 25 years. During one such lunch, Kathy Johnson described another, much larger group of her friends based on an even longer history of friendships, with their own ritual practices.

After becoming involved in a school musical production during their sophomore year at Washburn High School in South Minneapolis in the 1950s, 28 teenage girls bonded. One girl cajoled her friends to volunteer for the production and asked them to enlist others, with the result that 28 girls formed a lasting friendship group. They joined similar clubs (running many of them), "hung out" after school, and graduated on the same day. Eleven of the 28 still live in and around Minneapolis. Even though some moved away, they kept in touch with those still in Minneapolis when they came back to visit their parents.

During their high school years, the father of one girl jokingly called the group "The Foxes," a name that firmly stuck and continues to be what they call themselves. Contact with one another was sporadic until they decided to hold a reunion during the year they all turned 40 years old, and rented a lakeside lodge in northern Minnesota to meet for a "mega-sleepover." After its suc-

cess, they went on to hold a reunion every five years, spending four days and three nights together without husbands or partners, laughing and reminiscing. One member, Sandi Peaslee, a public school music teacher, composes a song for each reunion, now a ritual for them to learn and add to their repertoire of high school and "golden oldie" songs. For celebrating the year they turned 50 years old, she wrote, "The Foxes are Fifty, Isn't that a Kick?" In 1998, the year the friends reached their 60th birthday, a Fox who lived in Marblehead, Massachusetts, invited them to her home, with a side trip to Boston. In 2003, when they turned 65, they met in Portland, Oregon, where another member lived. Christina Lent, a reporter for the *Beaverton Valley Times,* followed them around to interview them for a feature story. Marna Reilly explicitly described her feelings about sisterhood in the group: "It's the love and sisterhood we share that is so important to me…. Some of us have known each other since we were five years old."

During each trip they bond by eating meals together, going sightseeing, and staying overnight for a sleepover, a teenage ritual. Of the original 28, two have died and another two or three have not participated in the outings. By 2005, the group kept in touch through e-mail, and the members have begun to plan their 2008 destination. Martha Michelson summarized the strong sentiment about their friendship and reunion rituals by saying, "We went on to have families and start careers. Through all of that, these friendships are my roots." Their long-lasting friendship gatherings are a mini rite of intensification for these women.

Another group, "The Fabulous Fürr Sisters," began in 1979 also in Minneapolis, according to professional costume designer Dawn D'Hanson, when three women who worked for the same theater company went shopping together. At Ragstock, a used-clothing store, each bought a vintage fur coat. That evening, they went to a club together wearing their furs; the club was cold, so they slipped back into their coats. Soon people stopped to ask if they were "in a group or something." In jest, they quickly concocted the name, "The Fabulous Fürr Sisters." It stuck beyond that first evening out, and initiated a ritual of affiliation. Shortly after that, one of the three Fürrs arrived at a work-related brunch meeting wearing antique 1940s clothing with correct accessories, including hat and gloves. This set the basic theme for later get-togethers. "Think *Casablanca,*" Dawn replied when queried about appropriate attire for Fürr events,

THEIR[S]…ARE RITUALS OF SEPARATION FROM THE REST OF THE WORLD AND ALLOW THEM TO OCCUPY A SOCIAL SPACE OF THEIR OWN, IN A TIME OF THEIR OWN CHOOSING.

"*Guys and Dolls.* Vintage." Their imagination ran wild, and the idea snowballed. Since 1979, they have dreamed up elaborate themes for ritual events, ranging from simple scavenger hunts held at members' homes, to a "Fürrs in Spurs" horse-riding outing. They also organized the "Fürrlympics," held every four years (zany affairs, such as the time three met at a backyard pool for the one and only event of synchronized swimming even though only one of them knew how to swim). There are now 12 active members; inactive members are referred to as "Frozen Fürrs" ("in cold storage"). Dawn says, "The Fürr Sisters aren't real—they exist in the 1940s." Each member chooses a fictitious name, one that starts with the letter F, with founding members answering to Fay,

Fern, and Frieda Fürr. The women hold quarterly meetings to establish "seriously silly" bylaws, as well as a yearly "Fürrvention" to vote on new members, referred to as "Fuzz pledges," and an annual "Frosted Fürr Ball" with cocktails, followed by dinner, a Grand March (to show off their vintage evening wear and introduce new members), dancing, and entertainment.

The Fabulous Fürr Sisters exemplify a sisterhood that erupted spontaneously and flourished, along with the development of their own rituals and ritualized behavior based on their playful fantasies. Their rituals are rituals of separation from the rest of the world around them, allowing them to occupy a social space of their own, in a time of their own choosing.

Sisterhood ritual behavior may develop within a temporary situation like that of contestants competing within a beauty pageant. For example, during the Miss America Pageant, the contestants live together for a short time. Although the pageant's purpose rests on winning the title of Miss America, bonding as well as rivalry can take place. On the night of Miss America's selection, all contestants vote for one woman to receive the title Miss Congeniality, and her award is announced publicly to the audience. At evening's end, when five finalists remain, they stand in a line waiting to hear who will become the winner, holding each other's hands. As the contestants are called in reverse rank order, "Fourth Runner-Up," "Third Runner-Up," to the final "Miss America," the women usually demonstrate affection. When one finalist leaves the stage, she embraces the woman next to her until only the winner is left. Of course, the winner accepts the crown from last year's Miss America with tears in her eyes, and then promenades down the runway, waving to the audience. This ritual is repeated from year to year with few, if any, changes, and demonstrates the act of sisterhood within a long-standing ritual of a rite of intensification for the community at large.

Formally organized rituals of sisterhood also exist in various forms around the world. One example includes religious orders that have developed rituals to train women for clerical service. A well-known group is the Poor Clare Sisters (the Poor Clares). In 2004, some 20,000 women were identified as Poor Clares, residing in more than 76 countries. Sisterhood in a religious group commits a woman to religious life, which includes prayer and service to others. Catholic sisters commit to serving Christ and leading a spiritual life within a circumscribed set of rules. The Poor Clares take the following vow:

"…to live in chastity, without anything of my own, in obedience and in enclosure, according to the Rule of the Poor Sisters of St. Clare which was approved by the Lord Pope Innocent IV and according to the Constitutions of the Order confirmed by the Holy See. In the service of God and the Church, I entrust myself with my whole heart to this religious family, so that by the grace of the Holy Spirit, through the intercession of the Immaculate Virgin Mary, our holy Father St. Francis, our holy Mother St. Clare and all the saints, and with the help of my sisters, I may fulfill my consecration."

To become a Poor Clare, a woman must contemplate and reflect on her reasons for changing her life, with a willingness to spend a period of time in "appropriate probation" with three stages that add to a minimum of six years. Probation includes being a postulant, a novice, and a person who professes to be bound by temporary vows. These stages have rituals attached that mark the significance of the woman's commitment as she becomes ever more deeply involved. A postulancy normally lasts one year and may be prolonged for no more than a second year. If judged suitable at the end of postulancy, an applicant puts her request to become a novice in writing. If she is accepted by the abbess and by a vote of the chapter members, the novice is recognized as beginning "her divine vocation" by serving for another two years. An important aspect of being named a novice is to surrender the wearing of secular dress. This ritual act separates the women from their former life. The rite of donning a religious habit demonstrates their willingness to be incorporated into a new life as a religious sister.

A WOMAN MUST CONTEMPLATE AND REFLECT ON HER REASONS FOR CHANGING HER LIFE, WITH A WILLINGNESS TO SPEND TIME IN "APPROPRIATE PROBATION."

After two years as novices, the women request admittance to profess temporary vows. The abbess decides on this step when backed by the vote of the members of the novice's local chapter. If admittance is approved, the Poor Clare takes the vows and serves another three years before final approval. When she is formally accepted as a Poor Clare, each woman devotes her life "to continue carefully [her] own spiritual, doctrinal, and practical formation." With this vow, she has become fully incorporated into her new status. In the materials describing the stages of commitment and acceptance into the order, the concept of living within the sisterhood is paramount. In answer to the question, "What is the most valuable lesson you have learned for growing and living in Community life," one sister declared, "I love community life, and I have never ceased to admire the virtues of the women with whom I live. I would hope to be as good as they are." Another woman said, "I find that being exposed to and accepting the wisdom and gifts of my sisters helps me to grow and expand in ways I wouldn't have otherwise."

Other formally organized groups of women that qualify as sisterhoods with rituals in the United States are the female auxiliaries to men's fraternal organizations, and college and university sororities. The female examples of Masonic orders include Eastern Star, Rainbow Girls, and Job's Daughters.

On college and university campuses, women-only groups, usually called sororities, are part of the Greek system of fraternities and sororities that unite under the umbrella organization, Panhellenic Council. An important part of sorority life is based on ritual, and there are several aspects of ritual. Initially, prospective members are "rushed," a term that covers the process of individuals visiting sorority groups in their sorority residence, if they have one, or another meeting place. At rush time, the prospective members assess the group in regard to whether or not they think they would like to join the sorority, and the group's members assess the rushees and consider whether or not to ask them to "pledge." When pledgeship is offered and accepted, a pledging ceremony follows, indicating the rushee's willingness to become a full member of the sorority after completing a pledge period, such as a college semester. A pledge goes through an initiation ceremony that confirms the affiliation and her separation from the non-Greek community. Both pledging and initiation ceremonies are carried out as rituals, and normally involve a particular item of dress, such as a special color garment or a pin. At the pledging ceremony, the formalized process allows the young woman to identify herself as being willing to become a "Greek." After the pledging ceremony, the individual goes through what anthropologist van Gennep termed a "period of transition," until she reaches full membership.

Whether living together in a local residence owned by the sorority or not, the women, having taken on full membership, are reminded regularly of their commitment to be "sisters." At the beginning of each weekly meeting, they hold an opening ritual. Each member repeats a secret oath, specific to that group. Some organizations also require a secret handshake to gain admittance to the room where the weekly meeting takes place. The stated purpose for accepting membership in Greek organizations is to promote friendships within the group through shared experiences and to demonstrate loyalty. For example, one women's Greek organization, Alpha Gamma Delta, has a purpose that reads: "To cultivate acquaintance with many whom I meet, to cherish friendships with but a chosen few, and to study the perfecting of those friendships." The emphasis on the lasting effects of becoming a sorority sister often extends beyond friendship and includes an ongoing commitment to the group's further stated purposes of leadership and service goals, and many undergraduates choose to continue their involvement as chapter alumnae to support the activities of the undergraduate chapter. Other opportunities to reaffirm sisterhood ties include meeting annually when each chapter holds a reunion of sisters, as well as participating in a national summer convention.

These sisterhood rituals illustrate the ways in which women develop ties to one another, sometimes establishing their own rituals or ritualized behaviors, and at other times joining those with preexisting, formalized rituals. Both kinds of ritual cement the bonds of sisterhood for a specific time and place.

SHIZUOKA, JAPAN / 1948

"IF YOU WANT SOMETHING DONE,

ASK A WOMAN."

— MARGARET THATCHER

QUITO, EQUADOR / 2001

THE GROOM'S SISTER PLAYS an important role in Hindu weddings, welcoming the bride to her new family. She may help her brother join the bride's sari to the groom's suit, or adorn the bride with flowers. /pages 132-133

FOR CENTURIES, THE DIVING GIRLS — *amas*—of Shizuoka, Japan, have collected *agar-agar,* a type of seaweed, from depths ranging from 10 feet to more than 30. Their diving ability binds them together in a unique sisterhood. /pages 134-135

OKLAHOMA CITY, OKLAHOMA / 1980

A BRIDE'S CLOSEST FEMALE FRIENDS and family help her dress for her wedding. The maid of honor and bridesmaids provide moral support before, during, and after the ceremony, in addition to performing other duties. /above left

SHARING BEAUTY TIPS, words of encouragement, and Vaseline, contestants for the title of Rodeo Queen in Oklahoma City, Oklahoma, forge friendships despite the competitiveness of the occasion. /above

DURING WORLD WAR II, silk and nylon stockings were extremely hard to come by. Women acted in concert to simulate the wearing of expensive hosiery, by painting seams down the backs of their legs. /page 138

UNITED STATES / 1940s

"When I'm good, I'm very good.

But when I'm bad, I'm better."

— Mae West

LONDON, ENGLAND / 1991

ALASKA / 1929

LIFELONG FRIENDS IN LONDON, England, meet weekly for Bingo, where they laugh about life, share stories about their families, and lean on each other for moral support as they weather growing old. /above left

TWO YOUNG INUIT GIRLS in an Alaskan village pore over the latest mail-order fashion catalog. Although these girls lived very different lives from their city counterparts, a shared interest in fashion connected them. /above

TRINIDAD AND TOBAGO / 1990s

WOMEN OF THE SHANGO Baptist faith celebrate Liberation Day with chanting, singing, and praying. They draw sustenance from the shared outpouring of faith and goodwill. /above left

IN THE HIGHLANDS of Guatemala, the women weave the traditional dress worn by men and women. Village- or ethnic-specific, the indigenous dress is still proudly worn. "I can't leave my dress, it's part of me," said one young woman. /below left

GUATEMALA / 1913

WOMEN IN HUTTERITE communities wear a simple kind of dress—long skirt, apron, and headscarf—that encourages a sense of togetherness and sets them apart from the outside world. /above right

FOR NYEPI, THE BALINESE New Year, women dressed in traditional attire go to temple with offerings for the gods. They have to ensure that all the rituals are properly observed. /below right

DURING JAPAN'S MEIJI period (1868–1912), physical education for girls was added to the school curriculum. The national ideal required healthy bodies for childbearing. /pages 144-145

Sisters in Arms

rooted in tradition

In two prior visits to Colombia in South America to cover the drug war in the mid-1990s, I had been warned by officials from both the American and the Colombian governments to beware of Marxist guerillas. Most feared were the FARC, the Revolutionary Armed Forces of Colombia, who were responsible for countless kidnappings and murders. Fortunately, we never had a run-in with the FARC. That all changed in August 1998.

The FARC had been a marginal group with some influence in rural areas. In the 1980s the group began to extort "taxes" from farmers growing coca, the shrub from which cocaine is obtained. The income allowed the guerillas to buy arms and recruit young people, and the FARC became a real threat. By 1986 drug traffickers—to protect their business—formed their own paramilitary group and, joining right-wing groups, mounted attacks against the FARC.

In 1998, Colombia's president, Andres Pastrana, invited the FARC to the negotiating table to discuss a peaceful solution. After months of back-and-forth discussions, and solemn declarations that the FARC had no involvement in drug trafficking, President Pastrana, in a historic move, ceded land the size of Texas to the FARC. The area, soon called the *Despeje*, or Demilitarized Zone, would be entirely administered by the group. FARC soldiers and associates began moving into the Despeje in droves. Journalists were invited in, and there began a period of relative calm—at least concerning the FARC—throughout the country.

On my third trip to Colombia, in 1998, the atmosphere seemed changed. In previous years, we'd drive through the country at high speeds to avoid confrontation with the FARC. This time, we traveled at a leisurely pace. As we got closer to the Despeje, we were met by an unlikely group of soldiers—perhaps 20 in all—at a checkpoint. They weren't wearing Colombian army fatigues, but a different military uniform. All of them carried assault rifles and had pistols strapped to their waists. They looked much younger than I expected. The most shocking thing was that more than half of them were women. They were the FARC, the very people we had grown to fear.

Although the FARC has maintained that their soldiers were volunteers who had to be over 18 years old, I could not help but wonder, after seeing such youthful faces, if those conditions had been met. The girls were thin and looked no more than 15. They hung out together, apart from the boys, who tried to project looks of authority.

Though they didn't smile much, I would hear the girls chatter and giggle among themselves. So many of the female soldiers who I had previously encountered—in Israel, the U.S., Mexico—always seemed as militant as their male counterparts. Not so the female FARC guerillas. I wasn't used to seeing female soldiers with pink lipstick and colored eyeliner. The adornments didn't end there. Most women wore their hair in ponytails held together by colorful ribbons or pretty barrettes. What caught my attention most immediately were the "Hello Kitty"-like key chains hooked to their AK-47 assault rifles. The same weapons that had in all likelihood been used to kill were also decorated with cartoon stickers. There was a sense of girliness and sisterhood that I had not expected. Had I not known of the extreme levels of violence—of abductions, torture, and killings—this group had perpetrated, I would have thought that the scene I was witnessing was … cute.

Once allowed into the Despeje, I was surrounded by other young female soldiers. There had been allegations that the FARC had pressured families into offering their children as payment for unpaid debt. A study conducted by Yvonne E. Keairns, Ph.D., entitled "The Voices of Girl Soldiers, Colombia," asserts that many female FARC soldiers are volunteers. Others suggested that girls sought out the guerillas to escape abusive families. Regardless of the individual reasons, almost all FARC soldiers came from poor families, and the FARC offered security and a future.

It was difficult to talk candidly with these women. Although they had been living in the jungle for years, the FARC had set up an impressive public relations machine. The women were under orders not to deviate from the party line. At times, older FARC commanders would tell the women what to say. When I asked some women why they joined the FARC, the commander through a female designee said, "The Colombian Government treats the majority unfairly, and we have become part of the FARC to liberate this land and bring freedom to the people."

Despite this hard front I began to witness, then to marvel at, the sisterhood that had developed within this community. They had separated from their families. They had been taught to kill, to serve as bodyguards, and to shield commanders. Yet they had bonded into a new sisterhood that rendered mutual support. In this militaristic environment they adhered to makeup and feminine hairstyles; they looked both full of teenage allure with their adornments, and professional in their FARC-issue uniforms.

Reports say that the FARC treated their female ranks more fairly than other guerilla groups. Incidents of rape were low, but girls were routinely given contraceptive injections to avoid becoming pregnant. They could have boyfriends and marry, but if they got pregnant, they would be obliged to have an abortion. It appeared that the rituals they were allowed to develop were carefully monitored. But those of sisterhood developed deeply, emotionally, on a level that could not be violated by their superiors.

I know little more of this community. In 2001, the FARC were found to be trafficking in narcotics. Colombia's new president, Alvaro Uribe, took the Despeje by force and drove the FARC back to the jungle, where it still operates.

—Lisa Ling

"WOMEN MAY BE THE ONE GROUP THAT

GROWS MORE RADICAL WITH AGE."

— GLORIA STEINEM

KURUÇAM, TURKEY / 2001

KURDISH WOMEN, all from the same tribe as indicated by their clothing, participate in and stand guard over the wedding ceremony of one of their own. Civil unrest has drawn Kurdish women into military service. /pages 148-149

GALILEE REGION, ISRAEL / 1995

SEGREGATED FROM THE MEN, Muslim women in Turkey draw strength from one another as they mourn over the body of a loved one. The segregation continues at the funeral service performed by the Imam at the mosque. /above left

AT THE FUNERAL for a slain Palestinian bus driver, women gather around his sister to lend physical and moral support in her grief. The women are urged to ululate in public to celebrate the death of a martyr. /above

IN SRI LANKA, YOUNG WOMEN groom one another for nits. This practice, which has sanitary origins, evolved into a social ritual that provides hours of uninterrupted time, in which they discuss the things that matter to them. /page 152

151

SRI LANKA / 1979

"A MINISTERING ANGEL

SHALL MY SISTER BE."

— WILLIAM SHAKESPEARE

BEAR ISLAND, NEW HAMPSHIRE / 2001

FALLS CHURCH, VIRGINIA / 2001

GIRLS OF CAMP NOKOMIS mourn the end of summer, taking consolation in possible reunion next year. Thousands of children participate in summer camps, forming lasting bonds of friendship through shared experiences. /above left

CHEERLEADERS LAUGH the night away at a slumber party in Falls Church, Virginia. Socialization outside the set hours and duties of the team solidifies team relationships, improves team spirit, and releases tension. /above right

THREE YOUNG GIRLS from the Rendre tribe in Nigeria return from market. They wear the traditional *cache-sexe* of their group. /page 157

155

"Maids are May, when they are maids,

but the sky changes, when they are wives."

— William Shakespeare

HARTSBURG, MISSOURI / 1990s

UNITED STATES / 1990s

THE BEAUTY PARLOR is an intimate place where women literally and figuratively let down their hair, sharing emotions, gossip, reminiscences, and idle chitchat while acquiring the "public face" that they wear to social events. /above left

IN A JOINT BEAUTY RITUAL, women try to project a desired image. The application of makeup has become such an integral part of being a woman that many feel naked going out in public without wearing at least lipstick. /above

PAPUA NEW GUINEA / 1977

KENYA / 1982

WOMEN OF THE GIMI TRIBE of Papua New Guinea decorate each other with fertility symbols for a prenuptial dance. They stage a ritual play (made up of several skits and/or dances) for initiations and weddings. /above left

THE CHALK MASKS and loose cloaks of these Pokot girls indicate that they are no longer girls, but not yet women, as they are preparing for initiation. The girls are sequestered for several weeks to learn how to be a woman. /above

MONGOLIA / 2002

TWO SISTERS of a nomadic family pose in their best robes. In Mongolia, most nomadic families are nuclear; many meet with their extended families at Naadam, a summer festival. /above left

GRAND BAY, DOMINICA / 1989

DRESSED IN WHITE DRESSES and veils, girls play before the Mass of their First Communion. The instruction leading up to the ritual, as well as the ritual itself, binds them together. /below left

TWO GEISHAS SLEEP carefully so that they do not disturb their makeup. Geishas undergo years of instruction in makeup, dress, and etiquette and move into a communal house. /above right

TWO WOMEN RINSE themselves after scrubbing with volcanic ash in a traditional bathhouse. Visiting the bathhouse in Russia is as much a social affair as a grooming ritual, where women eat, drink, and bathe. /below right

IN A MIME TO APPLY lipstick underwater, stunt swimmers at Wakulla Springs near Tallahassee, Florida, display the 1940s fitted bathing-suit style. One swimmer helps the other "primp" by holding up a compact mirror. /pages 164-165

KYOTO, JAPAN / 1990

MOSCOW, RUSSIA / 2000

WAKULLA SPRINGS, FLORIDA / 1944

"A SISTER IS BOTH YOUR MIRROR ——

AND YOUR OPPOSITE."

—— ELIZABETH FISHEL

BEIJING, CHINA / 1990s

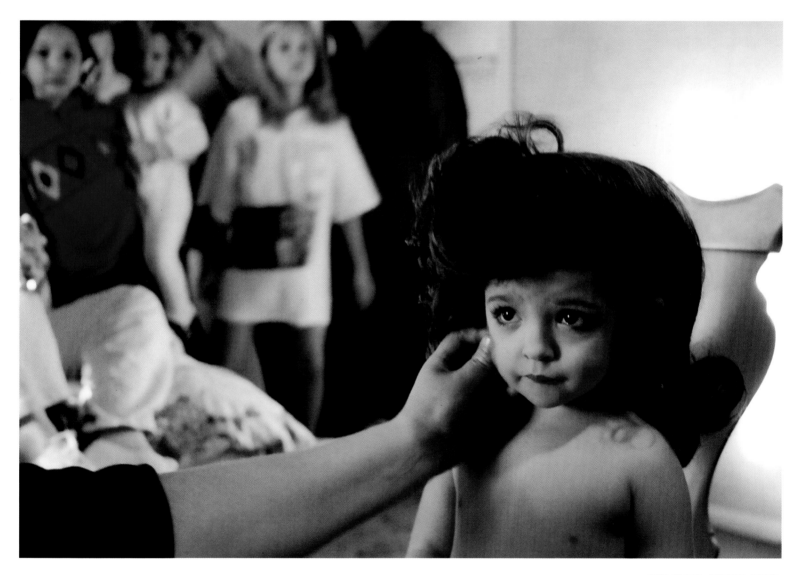

JEKYLL ISLAND, GEORGIA / 1990s

TO THE DESPAIR OF FEMINISTS, little girls world-wide find joy in playing with dolls. Some sociologists believe that role-playing with dolls teaches girls about gender, preparing them for their future roles as nurturers. /above left

A YOUNG GIRL IS PREPARED for the Universal Southern Charm Pageant. Proponents of child beauty pageants say that competition teaches girls social skills and valuable life lessons that will allow them to become successful. /above

167

Beneath the Headscarf
rooted in tradition

SINCE THE REVOLUTION OF 1979, WOMEN IN IRAN HAVE HAD TO ADHERE TO A STRICT ISLAMIC DRESS CODE WHENEVER THEY LEAVE THEIR HOMES. WOMEN HAVE TO COVER THEIR HEAD AND WEAR A LONG COAT; MAKEUP OR OTHER COSMETIC ADORNMENT IS ILLEGAL. FAILURE TO APPEAR IN PUBLIC PROPERLY dressed can result in severe punishment, including 76 lashes or imprisonment. Even foreign visitors must adhere to these rules. When I first visited Tehran, the Iranian capital, temperatures reached 110°F. I wasn't thrilled to have to conform to the dress code, but I didn't have a choice.

Wearing a headscarf and a long robe is a ritual for many Muslim women not only in Iran, but also in Western and other secularized countries. Some women simply wear a head covering because it is mandated by religious authority. Others wear it out of conviction. They don't see it as a restriction, but as a sign of modesty, and they feel they are not judged first by their appearance.

In Iran the rules for wearing the chador, the traditional robe, have been reversed more than once. In 1935, to modernize the country, Reza Shah Pahlevi, father of the last Shah, prohibited the chador. To wear it was punishable by a prison term. Iranian author Azar Nafisi wrote that her grandmother refused to leave the house for three months when she was forced to "unveil." Since that time, though, women have enjoyed fashionable, colorful dress. Wearing a headscarf became mandatory again in 1981, first in the workplace, then in the stores, finally in any public place.

In 1999 I covered the 20th anniversary of the revolution in Iran. One of my first stops was the tomb of the Ayatollah

Khomeini. Hundreds of people had gathered to celebrate and pay homage to the late leader. As in a mosque, men and women were separated, on opposite sides of the room, unable to see one another. The women's side looked like a sea of black ghosts in the floor-length black robes. I had not thought twice about the clear lip gloss that I had applied in the taxi before we arrived. Upon entering the room, I felt the gaze of dozens of women staring out of their black coverings. A group surrounded me, and one angry woman forcefully wiped the gloss from my mouth. At once the women fired off angry exhortations in Farsi. Though the language was unfamiliar, I understood. Wearing makeup is against the rules, and I broke them.

After the episode in Khomeini's tomb, I visited a nearby park and had a different experience. I noticed young women sporting coats far shorter and a lot brighter than the prescribed code. Girls in vibrant reds, blues, and purples rode their bicycles or jumped rope with friends wearing similar styles. Most shocking to me were the young women who had dared to dye their bangs blond, and now allowed several strands to peek out from under their headscarves. This small gesture made a bold statement. Something as seemingly trivial as dyeing their hair could get these girls arrested. Were they just being girly, or was this a ritual act of defiance? I wondered whether a subtle rebellion may be brewing among young women in protest to the strict Islamic dress codes. Were they creating a little niche of their own, a pocket of freedom and escape by subscribing to a forbidden beauty ritual? Most of them were born after 1979, and likely had far less knowledge of the revolution than generations prior. When I gathered a group together to chat, I was struck by the conversation. Almost all of them spoke English and were eager to talk to an American. They immediately fired off questions.

"Do you watch *Baywatch?*" a girl in red sunglasses asked.

"Do you think Metallica is cool?" asked a girl in faded blue jeans.

Soon we were discussing American pop culture in the middle of a park in the Islamic Republic of Iran. Still conscious of their surroundings, the girls would occasionally look over their shoulder to make sure that no official was watching. Such candor with a Western journalist could draw suspicion. Nevertheless, I couldn't get over the fact that in a country where books, magazines, and newspapers are heavily censored, and satellite television is illegal, we were talking about Pamela Anderson. How did they know who she was? After about an hour of idle chat, I finally got a chance to probe further.

"How are you celebrating the anniversary of the revolution?" I asked.

....pause....

"How are you remembering the Ayatollah Khomeini?" I pressed on.

....pause....

Then a girl with platinum blond streaks and Nike-like sneakers said, "Please do not ask us such questions."

I remembered a passage from Nafisi's best-selling book, *Reading Lolita in Tehran.*

"The streets of Tehran and other Iranian cities are patrolled by militia, who ride in white Toyota patrols, four gun-carrying men and women, sometimes followed by a minibus. They are called the Blood of God. They patrol the streets to make sure that women … wear their veils properly, do not wear makeup, do not walk in public with men who are not their fathers, brothers, or husbands."

I was suddenly wracked with guilt for having put them in an impossible situation, so I walked away.

During my stay in Iran, I talked with a few women behind closed doors. Iran is quite progressive when it comes to women in the workplace. Some of the women were very religious, some mildly so. The consensus, however, was that most of them would not stop wearing the traditional robes and scarves to cover up, even if they were allowed to dress as they pleased. Only a few of the younger women said they wouldn't mind having a choice.

—*Lisa Ling*

KABUL, AFGHANISTAN / 2002

ALTHOUGH MANY AFGHAN WOMEN cover up in public, they still take pride in their appearance and visit the beauty salon to get their hair styled. Work in beauty parlors is considered acceptable, as there is no contact with men. /above

HOPI INDIAN RESERVATION, ARIZONA / 1925

A YOUNG HOPI INDIAN MAIDEN sits quietly while a female relative arranges her hair in the traditional squash-blossom style. A symbol of fertility, the hairdo signifies that the girl has reached the age of maturity and marriage. /above

THANKS TO LONG HOURS spent dancing, stretching, and traveling together, the members of a ballet troupe in Jerusalem, Israel, form a close-knit community that functions very much like a family. /page 173

IN 1937 A DANCE CLASS at an all-women's college in Mississippi stages a living mural. Most higher education institutions in the United States were gender-defined until the social revolution of the 1960s and 70s. /pages 174-175

171

"CHANCE MADE US SISTERS,

HEARTS MADE US FRIENDS."

— ANONYMOUS

Self

ON PRESIDENT BILL CLINTON'S INAUGURATION DAY, HIS MOTHER, VIRGINIA KELLEY, DESCRIBED HER BEAUTY RITUAL TO PREPARE FOR THE BIG EVENT, INDICATING THAT SHE BEGAN EACH DAY IN THE SAME WAY: "THE FIRST THING I DO WHEN I SIT DOWN [AT MY DRESSING TABLE] IS PUT ON MY HAIR NET.... THEN I PUT IN MY

contacts. I don't have eyebrows so I have to draw them on, and I've found that contacts make putting on my eyebrows a lot easier. After the contacts, I wash my face. Fortunately, I have oily skin, so I don't have to waste time with cream.... I use the cheapest astringent I can find.... So I clean my face ... and get my bases: Max Factor, as cheap as you can buy. But it does the job, so I put that on and go over it with a wet sponge that has some pancake makeup on it."

After the pancake makeup, she applied eyeliner, attached false eyelashes and penciled in her eyebrows, then she added rouge and lipstick. "When it comes to lipsticks, I say the brighter the better. I have every color in the rainbow, and I match my lipstick color to my clothes." Virginia Kelley's beauty ritual exemplifies enhancing the self, a common and daily habit of women across the world even though many use different cosmetics and different practices. Enhancing the self emphasizes individuality, but the individual self exists within cultural boundaries and family expectations, often including what mothers taught their daughters. Oscar Wilde commented on the significance of beauty in *Picture of Dorian Gray*, a comment applicable across cultures:

"People say sometimes that beauty is only superficial. That may be so, but at least it is not so superficial as

Following a centuries-old tradition, a geisha applies her own makeup.

thought. To me, beauty is the wonder of wonders. It is only shallow people who do not judge by appearances. The true mystery of the world is the visible, not the invisible."

Within Western cultures, beauty rituals that relate to enhancing the self are easily visible and understood by looking at the world of models and beauty queens. Sarah Banet-Weiser, in conducting research on the Miss America Pageant, noted that the event "promotes a self-production that relies on a more complex interweaving of two themes of femininity: typicality and respectability." Furthermore, the purpose of the contest is as a scholarship competition. It was developed to attract a "certain class of girl," who could represent the nation by participating in this civic ritual.

Over the years, the interest in beauty pageants has encouraged the writing of how-to books with instructions about beauty rituals that emphasize individuality. Miss America of 1983, Debra Sue Maffett, reported that she became interested in local pageants during her college years, while working in a bakery to pay for college expenses. She entered many pageants and developed her untrained voice to participate successfully in the talent portion of each contest, and she learned how to dress and use makeup to her best advantage. In her book *Miss America Through the Looking Glass,* Nancy S. Martin disclosed techniques in common use by beauty pageant contestants, such as applying Vaseline to their lips and teeth to keep their lips moist and their teeth dazzling under television lights. The women use heavy makeup, hairpieces, and artificial eyelashes, and change or modify their hair color as each one tries to establish her singular identity. Such beauty practices become rituals within the larger calendrical rite of the Miss America Pageant, which itself is a rite of intensification.

The former chairman of the pageant, Albert Marks, declared "We stand for the great American middle class, the nonvocal middle class, for normal, average, young American womanhood." However, as each woman enters her first and then subsequent beauty pageants, she becomes fully aware of and carries out her interpretation of the expectations for beauty in preparing and presenting herself as an individual.

In anthropologist Arnold van Gennep's terms, this ritual involves separation of the contestants from the ordinary world as they enter into another social sphere, similar to Mende girls in Sierra Leone entering the Sande

THE CONTESTANTS EXIST IN A SOCIAL SPACE FAR REMOVED FROM EVERYDAY REALITY, AS EACH FOCUSES ON ENHANCEMENT OF HERSELF IN PREPARING TO MEET THE JUDGES.

encampment. Beauty pageants represent van Gennep's period of transition, because the contestants exist in a social space far removed from everyday reality, as each contestant focuses on enhancement of herself in preparing to meet the judges and face the audience. Each woman's beauty ritual—along with learning a proper walk, and presenting her body for display in a bathing suit and evening gown—combines with developing techniques to answer interview questions successfully. Each young woman hopes to achieve the significant distinction of wearing the crown.

Mende girls also follow beauty rituals and learn techniques. They know what is considered beautiful in regard to being a woman in their society, as described by

Sylvia Boone in *Radiance from the Waters: Ideals of Feminine Beauty in Mende Art:*

"A woman's face must be round, gently contoured.... The chin must be medium; too spread out has no firmness; sharp is ugly. High cheekbones are admired, and dimples on the cheeks or chin are considered charming. The ears, *ngoli,* should be small, close to the head, not large or protruding."

The author wrote 76 pages on "Physical and Metaphysical Aspects of Mende Feminine Beauty," listing and describing specific body parts and their desirable beauty characteristics for young Mende women. Her list began with beauty of the face and head, and included details for hair, forehead, eyes, nose, mouth, teeth, and neck. For beauty of the body, she listed further details for breasts, hands, hips and buttocks, genitals, thighs, legs, feet, skin color and texture. After enumerating desirable qualities for each specific part of the body, she pointed out that the overall look, "the complete picture," must come together as a whole. The Mende express the ideal size and proportion of a body with one word, *yengele,* meaning "delicacy:"

"Yengele relates to a small size that is complete and mature.... The yengele girl is petite yet rounded and well-shaped. She is graceful, finely balanced, dainty, wispy.... She is like a jewel, a tiny thing that is delicate, beautiful, precious. She is adored, admired, and desired."

Boone stated that a Mende girl must also have "beauty in the manner of doing things," meaning a proper facial expression, look, and gaze as well as a proper way of standing, sitting, kneeling, walking, and transporting objects. Boone provided additional details about Mende ways of behaving and of displaying proper self-comportment. She declared that the Mende people connect beauty and goodness:

"Mende expect women to be beautiful, graceful, delicate, curvaceous, pretty, clean, fresh, perfumed, groomed, adorned. And Mende expect women to be good, kind, sweet, patient, gentle, modest, loving, helpful, cheerful, honest, understanding. A beautiful girl must be a good girl."

These expectations for beauty in Mende women are indeed similar, almost equivalent, to the explicit and implicit expectations held for women who want to wear the crown as Miss America. In the early years of the Miss America Pageant, the judges used a formula of 100 total points regarding the body of each contestant:

Construction of head—15 points
Eyes—10 points
Hair—5 points
Nose—5 points
Mouth—5 points
Facial expression—10 points
Torso—10 points
Arms—10 points
Legs—10 points
Hands—10 points
Grace of bearing—10 points

Although the judging system has changed markedly over the years, judges still assess each woman for beauty of body and general gracefulness as she wears a swimsuit and an evening gown, displays a special talent, and responds to interview questions. Indeed, similar pageants based on Western expectations of beauty have developed in many countries, as described in the compendium *Beauty Queens on the Global Stage*. The Mende expectation that "a beautiful girl must be a good girl" exists in the United States as well. Expecting beauty and goodness simultaneously to exist became clearly evident when Vanessa Williams caused a scandal. Williams, as Miss America of 1984, was forced to step down after her photographs in the nude, taken before the national contest, were publicized. Even though she had won the crown and was deemed beautiful, such an act was not appropriate for Miss America, clearly illustrating that the concept of "a beautiful girl must be a good girl" is not unique to the Mende of Sierra Leone.

Far removed from either Western beauty pageants or Mende beauty expectations and related rituals are the worlds of widows. In some cultures, widowhood isolates the bereaving woman. A widow is singled out either by being excluded, or by being made the focus of the rituals related to the death of her husband, particularly at the time of the funeral.

Among the Kalabari of Nigeria for example, tradition demands that the widow separate herself from the rest of the mourners with a private ritual to show her sorrow. She is sequestered in a room by herself with little to eat or drink and cannot leave the room except for a specified time to sit by the corpse of her husband before his burial. At the final ceremony she must put in another appearance to sing a song that she composed in his honor. At his death, she shaves her head, and when her hair grows back, she pays little attention to grooming it or to other general grooming, including the use of cosmetics. She immediately wears black clothing, and continues to do so for two years. As time elapses, she can change to dark gray, and then to shades of gray, before returning to her regular garb. Her ritual emphasizes her separation from married life with her husband, indicat-

ing transition to the social space of ritual mourning.

In the 21st century, the prescriptions for dressing all in black have begun to change, and many widows have begun to wear white, said to be a Christian influence, and the time period for mourning has generally been shortened to six months.

Specific color requirements for clothing such as black and white are common throughout the world for widows to wear, usually being thought of as somber. The ritual of wearing black garments is followed by widows throughout the Mediterranean world. In India, white garments are the norm for Hindu widows. In addition, when her husband dies, a Hindu widow will remove the bangles from her wrists that are a sign of marriage. Expectations about appropriate wear at funerals become explicit in many situations. In his research on the death rituals in a rural Greek village, Loring Danforth wrote that women in mourning are expected to dress completely in black, including a black kerchief to cover their hair, forehead, and neck.

"The length of time a woman wears black is determined primarily by her relationship to the deceased. A widow should wear black for the rest of her life, or until she remarries, something she should not do before the [final rite] for her husband. The mother of a young child who dies should wear black for five years or longer. At the death of a parent or sibling a woman should wear black for a period of one to five years, at the death of a mother-in-law or father-in-law for one year. A woman whose aunt or uncle has died would be expected to wear black for six months, whereas a 40-day mourning period would suffice at the death of a more distant relative."

Special garments clearly identify a formal mourning period, acknowledging that each woman goes through a transition that marks an end to a significant relationship with a person no longer alive. In some traditions, a specified garment color may not be the only requirement for a widow's appropriate dress. For example, a popular press account reproached Jackie Kennedy Onassis when she arrived at Aristotle Onassis's funeral on the island of Skorpios, indicating that her dress for the occasion severely violated Greek custom. One observer attending the funeral said:

"When she [Jackie Onassis] took off the long coat she was wearing, I saw that beneath it, she had on an old

IN SHIFTING FROM MOURNING GARB TO ORDINARY CLOTHING, SHE INDICATES THAT CULTURALLY SHE IS AGAIN AVAILABLE FOR MARRIAGE.

black skirt, a sweater, and flesh-colored stockings. And in the worst possible taste, she wore a gold necklace and other jewelry—something that's never done when Greeks are in mourning."

Another mourner made similar comments and confirmed that Jackie was inappropriately dressed: "It is improper for a widow to wear jewelry and light colored stockings at a memorial service. This is a custom strictly adhered to in the Greek Church."

In some cases, as in the Greek village example, a widow no longer needs to wear her mourning clothes after the stipulated time. In shifting from mourning garb to ordinary clothing, she indicates that culturally she is again available for marriage. In other cultural cases, however, she must continue to wear prescribed mourning ensembles, signaling a permanent state of widowhood with no possibility for remarriage. In van Gennep's terms, the ritual of mourning in the latter example, beginning with a formal ceremony such as a funeral, separates her from wifehood; she then becomes incorporated into a continuing state of widowhood.

Life changes for most women when they become widows and are single again. Life also changes for single women when they become homeowners because the ritual act of buying a house has traditionally been thought to be part of starting or having a family. Today, an emerging ritual for single women that focuses on the self in the United States is the purchase of a house, town house, or condominium, without marriage looming on the horizon. A news feature of the Twin Cities' *Star Tribune* dated May 14, 2005, reported that single women "are now the second largest group of home buyers behind married couples." Within the last two decades, the numbers of women homeowners have nearly doubled to almost 20 percent of all home buyers. Perhaps most surprisingly, in 2004, single men represented only 8 percent of all buyers. No clear reason for the difference was indicated, but the conjecture arose that men were more likely than women to remain roommates longer or to live at home without paying rent. Or they may not be as focused on their financial futures.

Certainly we can perceive a ritual process in the series of actions related to becoming a homeowner, for homeowners separate themselves from those in the community who do not own property, thus being technically free to move. When committing to becoming a homeowner, buyers proceed through the liminal, or transition, stage from renter to buyer by proving that they have the resources to make a down payment, and acceptable credit that indicates the ability to make monthly payments.

Traditionally, the purchase of a house was related to establishing a family, such as when a couple gets married or later on when the family includes offspring. In many cases a home purchase has represented a commitment to community and a job, with one's family intending to stay and put down roots. Often the incorporation phase of the ritual of homeownership is emphasized when a house-warming party takes place, and friends and relatives come to celebrate with the new homeowners as they are moving into their home.

Jim Buchta, the reporter of the *Star Tribune,* quoted Marni Hockenberg, who said she used to think that homeownership was only for the betrothed, but she bought a house after renting for more than ten years. "'If a woman bought a home on her own back then, you were looked upon like an ultra, ultra-independent woman who was not marriage material,' said Hockenberg, now almost 50 years old and divorced." Examples like these indicate that attitudes about single women owning homes and being independent have changed markedly in the past few years, not just the demographics regarding divorce and the fact that young people are getting married later in life.

Faith McGown, a real estate agent in Edina, Minnesota, who specializes in selling houses to single females, reported that one of her buyers cried, but not with tears of joy, when she signed her purchase agreement. She had always "thought she would be married or with someone." Even though she found it hard to accept the idea that she was alone, "she didn't want any more time to go by without owning a home."

When a single woman becomes a homeowner, she focuses on herself, but she does not necessarily isolate herself from others. Some ritual actions, however, may involve solitude or socially prescribed isolation, such as the act of prayer.

Prayer exists in a variety of religions: Christianity, Islam, Judaism, Hinduism, Buddhism, and many indigenous beliefs. People may pray together in a group, or single individuals may pray alone. The ritual of prayer involves communication with the divine whether verbally or nonverbally offered, and certain causes and occasions appear particularly to appeal to women, such as prayers for peace and justice and to end violence.

For Hindus, public temples exist, and most homes hold small altars or worship rooms. But Hindus gener-

IN DAILY LIFE I PRAY AND MEDITATE FOR HALF AN HOUR IN THE MORNING. IF I DO IT WITH CONCENTRATION, I CAN FEEL THE MENTAL CALM FOR THE WHOLE DAY.

ally do not meet regularly for organized religious services (except perhaps on special occasions such as the birthday of a god like Krishna or Rama). Making *puja* involves thanking the universe and making personal requests for blessings through a ritual of lighting oil lamps, burning incense, ringing a bell or bells, and calmly reciting sacred verses in a place set aside. Because women normally take charge of household and family affairs, they frequently make puja. Bharat Parekh, a scholar born in India and raised in a Hindu family, who lives in the United States, suggested that perhaps those women who like ritual prefer doing puja, whereas those who like emotional release prefer playing an instrument or singing, and those who like intellectual exchange are more drawn to spiritual discourse with a pundit or guru (a wise person or a teacher). In still another Indian example, village women decorate their houses with "painted prayers," an act to bring a blessing to the house. As Stephen Huyler reported in *Painted Prayers: Women's Art in Village India*:

"Everywhere in India, Hindu women regularly paint their homes as part of religious ritual. The wall and floor decorations of Indian women are usually ephemeral, remaining hours, days, or weeks before being worn off by the abrasion of activity or weather and replaced by new interpretation of design. In some areas this decoration is very frequent; daily in the far south … or weekly in eastern India. Elsewhere it is done less often. Women throughout India herald important occasions either by repainting their entire houses or by decorating auspicious portions of them."

The occasions chosen for painting mark holy festivals for special gods and goddesses, seasonal changes, or significant family events from birth to death. The visit of an important guest or the return of a woman's adult offspring may also warrant her artwork.

An insight into the place of prayer in one woman's life comes from a Buddhist nun as part of her account of committing to a religious life:

"In my daily life, I pray and meditate for half an hour in the morning. If I do it with concentration, I can feel the mental calm for the whole day. Still, I need more time and a quiet place to practice the teachings intensively to be able in a future life to gain enlightenment for the benefit of all sentient beings."

Another woman, from a different religious perspective, Hibba Abugideiri, a professor at George Washington University, was born in the Sudan and brought up in the United States in Indianapolis, Indiana. She disclosed that her faith as a Muslim woman involved talking to God:

"The Qur'an does not speak only to men. It speaks, quite explicitly, to women. I knew this at a young age, not because I read the Qur'an, but because I talked to God all the time. I knew with certainty that He responded. Maybe this spiritual consciousness was the result of my Sufi ancestry; my grandfather and father were Sufis of the popular Tijaniyyah order in Sudan. Sufism has historically welcomed women's spiritual connection to God. Or maybe it was because it never occurred to me that my gender could impede a relationship with God. Those conversations taught me that intellect was connected to faith. As an adult, I found it unreasonable that God would prefer men to women in anything, but especially in terms of worshiping Him."

The concept of each woman as a self differs from culture to culture, whether we analyze rituals that relate to beauty practices, widowhood, or prayer. At one extreme is the example of an individual with a strong commitment to the "good of the group," like Japanese kamikaze pilots or Palestinian terrorists acting as human bombs. In other examples, emphasis on individualism, as among American entrepreneurs, provides the opposite philosophy: The self is paramount. Even these examples of "self," however, are bounded by how an individual woman interprets what culturally is prescribed for her by her community, her family, and her sisterhood.

Van Gennep's ideas relating to rituals for an individual as a rite of passage, and the idea of rituals being important to community solidarity provide us ways to think about the significance of individual women's rituals in societies throughout the world.

BANGKOK, THAILAND / 1988

CALCUTTA, INDIA / 2001

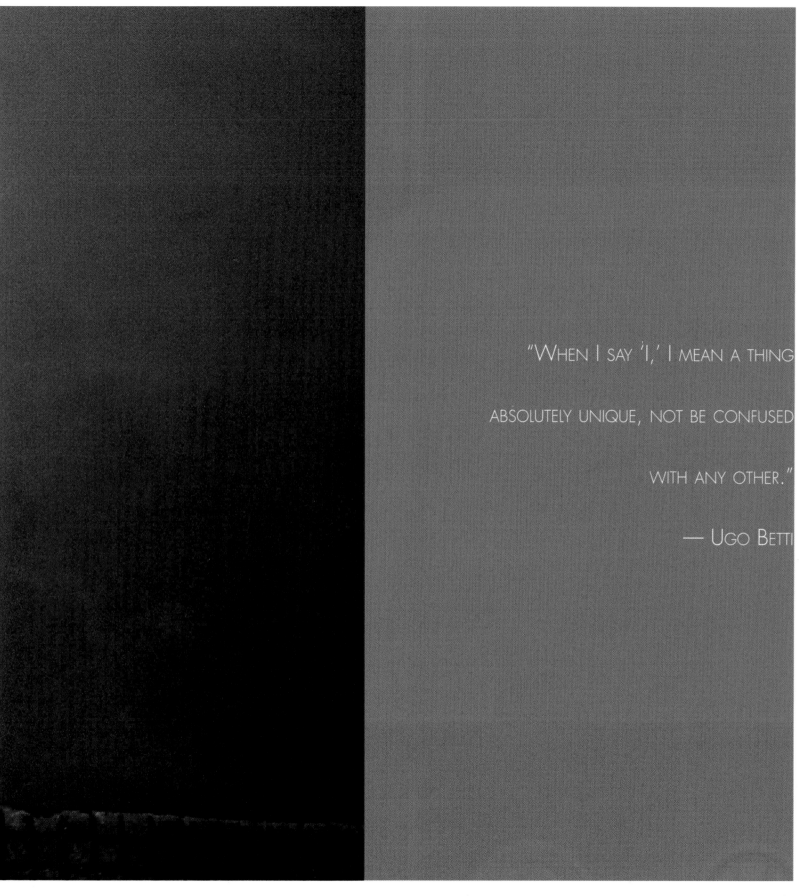

"WHEN I SAY 'I,' I MEAN A THING

ABSOLUTELY UNIQUE, NOT BE CONFUSED

WITH ANY OTHER."

— UGO BETTI

SARATOGA SPRINGS, NEW YORK / 1993

UNIFORMED STUDENTS of the Assumption Convent girls' school in Bangkok pay homage to their teachers. School uniforms are said to increase students' self-confidence without the social dictates of fashion. /pages 184-185

TYSONS CORNER, VIRGINIA / 2002

A WOMAN IN CALCUTTA untangles her hair after washing it in a canal. Though modest, many women in India routinely bathe in public. They learn at an early age to expertly wash themselves while fully dressed in a sari. /pages 186-187

THE RELAXING, EFFERVESCENT mineral waters of Saratoga Springs, New York, soothe and ease the body. Women have been coming to the Lincoln Mineral Baths since 1915 to rejuvenate, hoping to eradicate the effects of time. /above left

IRONICALLY, WHILE MANY WOMEN would object to swimming through a bed of seaweed, they readily encase their body in seaweed wraps to detoxify, tone, and hydrate their skin so that they appear more beautiful. /above

NAMPULA PROVINCE, MOZAMBIQUE / 1992

A **MAKUA WOMAN** from Madagascar wears a *mascara de beleza*—mask of beauty—noted for its skin softening properties made from *musiro,* an extract from the roots of a native plant. /above left

COSMETIC SURGERY is more popular than ever as women seek to reach a self- or society-imposed level of perfection. In 2004, more than 10.7 million procedures were performed on women in the United States. /below left

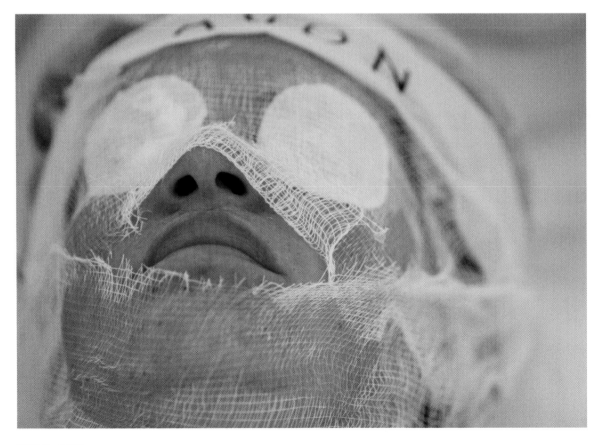

VIRGINIA / 2000

DECORATIVE PAINT COVERS the face of this Papua New Guinea woman at Garoka's annual sing-sing. Her costume, which also includes shell necklaces and feathers, celebrates her tribe's heritage and her country's independence. /above right

GAROKA, PAPUA NEW GUINEA / 1998

HANGING AT THE CENTER of the forehead, where the *ajna*, or preservation, chakra resides, the *maang tikka* pendant is worn by a Hindu bride to indicate her willingness to "preserve," the genes of the groom. /below right

THE HAIR STYLE — two braids formed in the shape of "wings" and wrapped in silver—and apparel and jewelry of this Mongol woman denote her status as a high-ranking, married member of society. /page 193

"WOMEN ARE THE ONLY EXPLOITED

GROUP IN HISTORY TO HAVE BEEN IDEALIZED

INTO POWERLESSNESS."

— ERICA JONG

IRAN / 1999

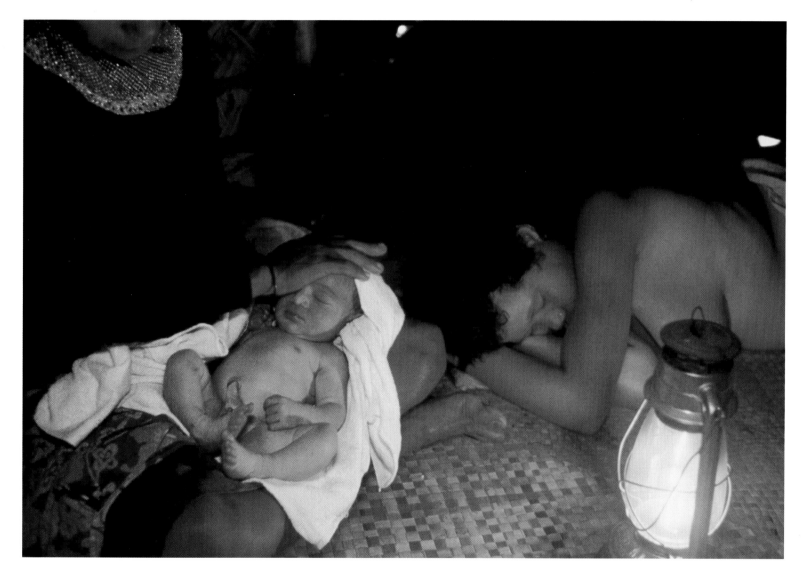

TROBRIAND ISLANDS, PAPUA NEW GUINEA / 1992

IN IRAN, A MIDWIFE listens to a patient's belly. In the past, the Muslim midwife arrived on foot and coached the mother during birth. She stayed on beyond the birth, participating in a weeklong celebration. /above left

A MALAY WOMAN RESTS after giving birth, while the midwife tends to the baby. In the matrilineal society of the Trobriand Islands, pregnancy is revered. Pregnant women are pampered and accorded every privilege. /above

Bodyworks *rooted in tradition*

THROUGHOUT HISTORY WOMEN HAVE SOUGHT WAYS TO ENHANCE THEIR APPEARANCE. ARCHAEOLOGISTS HAVE FOUND MIRRORS AND MAKEUP KITS AMONG THE EARLIEST SOCIETIES. WOMEN APPLIED POWDERS AND PAINTS, WAXES AND OILS, AND ANY NUMBER OF SECRET LOTIONS AND POTIONS TO LOOK MORE attractive, and they used clothing and accessories to lift, squeeze, or pad the body.

Some of the more extreme measures involved complete alterations of the body. The Padaung women of Burma, for example, were famous for their long necks. Here, mothers played a role in maintaining a ritual for their daughters to make them as alluring as possible for an advantageous marriage. A mother applied a new brass ring to her daughter's neck every two years from age five on, stretching the neck by 10 inches. As a result, four thoracic vertebrae were pulled up into the neck. This caused such severe changes that a women could no longer hold up her head when the rings were removed in old age.

Another practice, going back to ancient China's Tang dynasty, is foot-binding. I happened to be a guest on the *Oprah Winfrey Show* on a day when her book club chose to discuss Pearl S. Buck's novel *The Good Earth*, and the common practice of that period of foot-binding. I was there to talk about an entirely separate topic, though, coincidentally, one of my great-grandmothers had had bound feet.

Between the years of 920 and 1911, it was customary and considered attractive for Chinese women to have their feet bound. Mothers with bound feet performed the ritual on their daughters: At about age five, mothers would wrap their daughters' feet in ten-foot-long bandages, forcing the small toes under the sole of the foot. This process broke the arch of the foot and, by binding ever more tightly, gradually decreased the size of the child's foot. Within two years the foot could be stuffed into tiny shoes smaller than the girl's palm. The feet were left distorted and deformed. Nevertheless, men seemed to find them irresistible, as they were representative of femininity and delicacy. As a result of this practice, older women were often unable to walk without a cane, if they could walk at all.

Talk of foot binding today inspires sneers and confusion. As we discussed the topic on Oprah's show, I looked up to see audience members wearing looks of utter perplexity. As a woman whose maternal grandmother's feet were bound to the point of debilitation, I often ask myself how a woman who had gone through this ordeal herself could be compelled to perform such a horrific and painful procedure on her daughter.

Beauty rituals continue in extreme ways to this day. The evening after taping that episode of Oprah's show, I watched a hugely popular American TV show called *The Swan*. The show is a beauty pageant typical of any other in the world, except that all contestants have to undergo extreme levels of cosmetic surgery to the point where they are totally unrecognizable from their original self.

Women suffer through injections that paralyze the forehead to fill in wrinkles, liposuction that draws fat out of the stomach and redistributes it to the buttocks, silicone implants that increase breast size, and shaved cheekbones to make the face narrower. These procedures have become so commonplace that we rarely blink when hearing about someone who has "gone under the knife." Visit any upscale café on the Upper East Side of Manhattan and at least a handful of women have "had some work done."

Plastic surgery has reached near-epidemic levels all over the world. In some Asian nations, however, women are having cosmetic operations not just to maintain their youthfulness, but rather, to look more Western. It's become so widespread that the faces of Korean women are literally changing. Asians are known for their almond-shaped eyes without creases in the eyelids. In an effort to achieve more rounded-looking eyes, record numbers of Korean women are having their eyelids cut.

It's difficult to get Korean women to speak openly about their surgery. Many women who have had cosmetic operations destroy their "before" pictures, and neglect to tell their husbands even after they've married. But if asked broadly about how common it is for women to have cosmetic surgery, one would be hard-pressed to find anyone who would deny that the practice is highly pervasive.

The women with whom I spoke told me that there is a great push in Korean society to conform to a certain look to get a job and find a husband. Cultural pressures of achieving a certain beauty ideal thus engender new rituals not only for an advantageous marriage, but also for success in the workplace.

It's been reported that high school girls as young as 14 are heading to plastic surgeons' offices in droves. It's happening with such frequency that a *Time* magazine article by Chisu Ko says, "kids drop into the plastic surgeon's office after school, and when they get home their folks can barely recognize them."

In Seoul, I was astounded by the great number of plastic surgery clinics—at least two centers on every street. I was invited to a tea party with ten young Korean mothers, half of whom had had some work done; only one had told her husband. Fascinated by these statements and armed with a video camera, I asked if I could interview the group about the popularity of cosmetic surgery in Korea, and why they had chosen to do it. It was as if I had asked how many men they had been involved with sexually. They shyly covered their mouths and said they didn't want anyone to know that they had gone through this ritual. The one woman who agreed to an interview was the woman whose husband knew. His profession: plastic surgeon.

—*Lisa Ling*

CHINA / 2000

SHANGHAI, CHINA / 1994

OUTLAWED IN 1911, the Chinese custom of foot-binding, resulting in tiny feet, first gained popularity in the Tang dynasty around A.D. 920, after Emperor Li Yu ordered his concubine to bind her feet and dance. /above left

IN SHANGHAI, a 62-year-old woman's need to provide for her family prompts her to undergo cosmetic surgery so that she will appear younger and more attractive, enabling her to return to work. /above

MEXICO / 1977

HONOLULU, HAWAII / 1998

IN MEXICO, as a sign of welcome, respect, fruitfulness, and transition, the wife of an outgoing Huichol Indian governor crowns the spouse of the incoming leader with gifts of cigarettes, cheese, and fruit. /above left

A CONTESTANT PREPARES for the Miss Universe Pageant. A cast of characters supports and enhances each entrant's beauty, decorum, and talent, striving to match society's ideal of the perfect woman. /above

DEFIANT AND PROUD, this young pregnant Hesquiat Indian woman of Vancouver Island in Canada wears the cedar-bark hair ornaments normally donned by young girls on the fifth day of their puberty ceremonies. /pages 202-203

VANCOUVER ISLAND, BRITISH COLUMBIA, CANADA / 1910

"IT TAKES A LOT OF COURAGE TO SHOW

YOUR DREAM TO SOMONE ELSE."

— ERMA BOMBECK

HAINAN ISLAND, CHINA / 1938

204

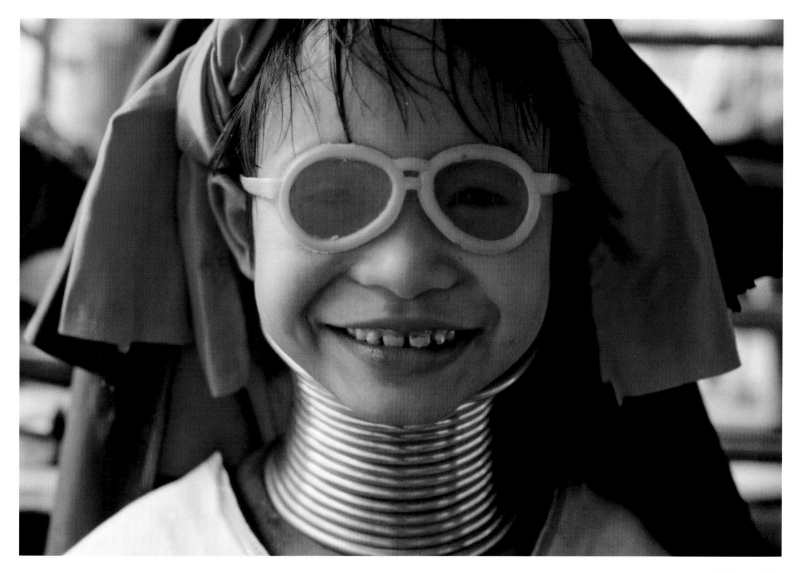

THAILAND / 2000

THE FIVE-POUND BRASS EARRINGS of this girl denote her high rank in the Li society of Hainan Island in the South China Sea. No longer worn, the earrings were normally swung up on the head to alleviate their weight. /above left

THE KAREN PADAUNG WOMEN of northern Thailand pride themselves on a long neck, a custom only rarely in use today. A girl receives her first brass ring at the age of five and has another added every other year. /above

205

OMO VALLEY, ETHIOPIA / 2000

RHODE ISLAND / 1994

TO THE KARO PEOPLE OF ETHIOPIA, scarred women are considered particularly sensual and attractive. The body scarification on this woman illustrates her strength and resistance to disease. /above left

A GOLDEN TAN REPRESENTS HEALTH, vitality, and beauty to millions of women in Western society. This notion began in the 20th century, when a tan became a symbol of wealth and leisure, reversing a preference for pale skin. /above

AT A LEGAL BROTHEL IN NEVADA, a prostitute and a prospective client engage at the bar. Following an unspoken code of conduct, discussion of the business terms and transactions only occur behind closed doors. /pages 208-209

A MOORISH WOMAN stands in the doorway of a house in Algeria. Her provocative pose and dress actively advertise her status in society. /left

AS A SIGN OF BEAUTY, the Ainu of Japan began tattooing a girl's mustache when she was two or three years old. This practice was outlawed at the turn of the 20th century. /right

AT A WHEAT-BLESSING CEREMONY in Hungary, a woman's dress expressed her married status: Unmarried women wore white dresses and head pieces; married women had colorful costumes and unadorned hair. /page 212

A YANOMAMI INDIAN GIRL from the northern Amazon forest wears the traditional ornamental *palloitos*—little sticks. /pages 214-215

A HULI DANCER OF GAROKA, Papua New Guinea, performs a dance at a tribal sing-sing, adorned with light-colored clays to indicate mourning and death. /page 217

A ZULU SONGOMA, or medicine woman, performs a thank-you dance for a man who brought her a wildebeest tail, an important element in ceremonies. /pages 218-219

HUNGARY / 1929

"A MODEST WOMAN, DRESSED OUT IN ALL

HER FINERY, IS THE MOST TREMENDOUS

OBJECT OF THE WHOLE CREATION."

— OLIVER GOLDSMITH

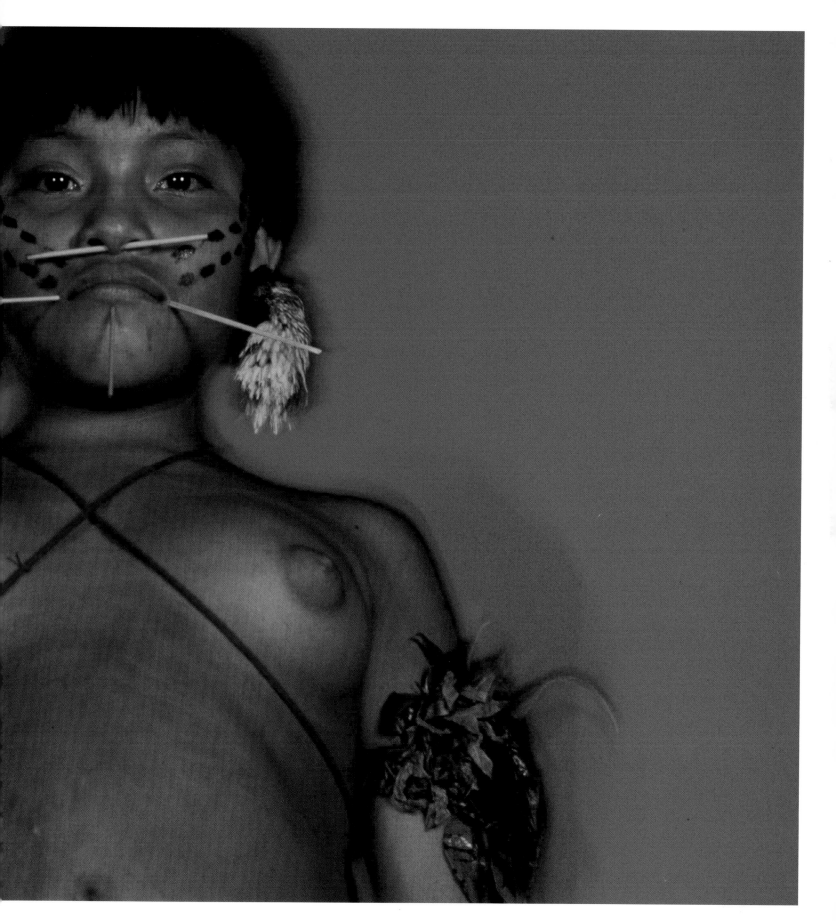

"Free your hair,

and the rest will follow."

— Lorraine Massey

GOROKA, PAPUA NEW GUINEA / 2000

KWAZULU-NATAL PROVINCE, SOUTH AFRICA / 1994

INDEX ～

ADDITIONAL READING

Anderson, M. and Peek, P. (Eds.) (2002). *Ways of the Rivers*. University of California / Argyrou, Vassos. (1996). *Tradition and Modernity in the Mediterranean: The Wedding as Symbolic Struggle*. Cambridge University Press / Baldizzone, T. and Baldizzone, G. (2001). *Wedding Ceremonies: Ethnic Symbols, Costume, and Rituals*. Flammarion; Banet-Weiser, S. (1999). *The Most Beautiful Girl in the World: Beauty Pageants and National Identity*. University of California Press / Bell, C. (1997). *Ritual: Perspectives and Dimensions*. Oxford University Press / Bhandari, V. and Kashyap, R. (1999). *Celebrating Dreams: Weddings in India*. Prakash Books / Bivans, A.-M. (1991). *Miss America: In Pursuit of the Crown*. MasterMedia Limited / Boone, S. (1986). *Radiance from the Waters: Ideals of Feminine Beauty in Mende Art*. New Haven, Yale University Press / Cohen, C., Wilk, R., and Stoeltje, B. (Eds.) (1996). *Beauty Queens on the Global Stage: Gender, Contests, and Power*. Routledge / Cooper, Sue Ellen. (2004). *The Red Hat Society: Fun and Friendship After Fifty*. Warner Books / Duff, S. (1983). *The Miss Universe Beauty Book: You can be a Pageant Winner or Look Like One*. Coward-McCann, Inc. / Danforth, L. (1982). *The Death Rituals of Rural Greece*. Princeton University Press / Edia Canter, Norma. (1999, April). *"La Quincearera: Towards an Ethnographic Analysis of a Life Cycle Ritual"* In *Southern Folklore*. http://colfa.usta/cantu/quincearera.html / Eicher, J. and Erekosima, T. (2002). *"Fitting Farewells: The Fine Art of Kalabari Funerals."* In *Ways of the Rivers*, Anderson, M and Peek, P. (Eds.) (2002). University of California / Griffing, M.F. (1981). *How to be a Beauty Pageant Winner*. Simon & Schuster / Haynes, M. (1998). *Dressing up Debutantes*. Berg: Oxford / Kelley, V. C. (1994). *My Life Leading with my Heart*. Pocket Star Books / Lamp, F. Book Review of Boone, S. *Radiance from the Waters*. In *African Arts*. February, 1987, V. XX, no. 2. / Lynch, A. (1999). *Dress, Gender, and Cultural Change*. Berg: Martin, N.S. (1985). *Miss American Through the Looking Glass: The Story Behind the Scenes*. Simon & Schuster, Inc. / Moreno, J. (2005). *"Latino Style."* Perani, J., and Smith, F. (1998). *The Visual Arts of Africa: Gender, Power, and Life Cycle Rituals*. Prentice Hall / Poor Clares. (2005). http://www. poorclare.org/; Salcedo, M. (1997). *Quinceanera!* Henry Holt & Co / Steele, V. (Ed.) (2005). *Encyclopedia of Clothing and Fashion*. Thomson Gale / Sweet 16. (2005). http://www.mtv.com /onair/dyn/ sweet_16/series.jhtml / Turner, V. *The Ritual Process* / van Gennep, A. (1960.) *The Rites of Passage*. Routledge and Kegan Paul. *Girls on the Verge: Debutante Dips, Gang Drive-bys, and Other Initiations*. St. Martin's Press / Visona, M. (2001). *A History of Art in Africa*. Prentice Hall, Abrams.

BIOGRAPHIES

JOANNE B. EICHER, Regents Professor of the Department of Design, Housing and Apparel at the University of Minnesota, teaches and conducts research on the cultural aspects of dress, with particular interest and expertise in Asia and Africa. She conducted research in West Africa, particularly in Nigeria, and has lectured in the U.S., Europe, Africa, and Asia. She co-authored the recent text, *The Visible Self* (2000), on the significance of dress, and edited or co-edited the following books: *Fashion Foundations: Early Writings on Dress* (2003), *Dress and Gender* (1992), *Dress and Identity* (1995), and *Beads and Beadmakers* (1998). She was a consultant and wrote an introduction for *National Geographic Fashion* (2001), and has published widely in professional journals. She is consulting editor for Berg Publishers (Oxford, England), for the Dress, Body, Culture book series, and an Associate Editor for Scribner's three-volume *Encyclopedia of Clothing and Fashion* (2005). She has been selected as Editor-in-Chief for a ten-volume *World Encyclopedia of Dress and Adornment* for Routledge, to be published between 2007 and 2012. She lives in St. Paul, Minnesota.

LISA LING is the first woman host of the the award-winning documentary series *Explorer*, on the National Geographic Channel, since the series' premiere two decades ago. For *Explorer*, Ling has covered the looting of antiquities in war-torn Iraq, investigated the deadly drug war in Colombia, examined complex issues surrounding China's one-child policy, and explored the phenomenon of female suicide bombers in Chechnya and in Israel's occupied territories. In 2005 she revealed the dangerous culture inside American prisons. Prior to joining *Explorer*, Ling was known for revealing her "view" of the world to millions of Americans as co-host of Barbara Walters' daytime talk show *The View*. Ling is also a special contributor to *The Oprah Winfrey Show*, in which role she has traveled from India to the Congo. Ling has worked in television for 15 years. At age 16, the Northern California native hosted *Scratch*, a nationally syndicated teen magazine show. She then became one of the youngest reporters for Channel One News, a network seen in middle and high schools across the country. Later, as its senior correspondent, she visited hotspots around the globe, hunting down cocaine processing labs, reporting on refugee crises, and sharing tea with the Dalai Lama. Her position as a role model for today's youth is one that she embraces. She lives in New York City.

ACKNOWLEDGMENTS

Joanne B. Eicher thanks those who brainstormed at the dawn of this project on women's rituals: M. Janice Hogan, Frank Miller, Margaret Deppe, Katalin Medvedev, Remi Douah, Barbara Heinemann and Mary Alice Chaney. Margaret Deppe provided support and references throughout the writing along with Megan Wannarka. Generously and graciously, several shared personal examples that greatly enhanced the chapters: Tassoula Hadjiyanni and her parents Katerina and Zacharias Hadjiyanni; Meriem Chida, her parents Mahmoud and Rachida Chida, and her aunt Zina Chida; Kathryn Johnson and "The Foxes;" Dawn D'hanson and the "Fabulous Fürr Sisters;" Maychoua Lo, Masami Suga; Jeong-Ju Yoo; Bharat Parekh; Hazel Lutz; Cynthia Becker; T. V. Erekosima; and Ibiso Erekosima.

I would like to thank my mentor Mitchell Koss for teaching me everything I know about journalism. To David Royle, Executive Producer of "Ultimate Explorer," thank you for your committment to telling vitally important, ignored stories. Finally, I am deeply grateful to Jill Van Lokeren, Ellen Rakieten and Oprah Winfrey for allowing me to bring issues that no other TV outlet thinks "will rate" to the forefront. That's why *Oprah* continues to be the best there is.

—Lisa Ling

National Geographic wishes to thank Bill Bonner, Director of the Photographic Archive, who aided in picture research; and Carolyn Herter, who created the original concept and outline for this book.

Lines reprinted with kind permission by the publishers from

Baldizzone, T. and Baldizzone, G. (2001) Wedding Ceremonies, Paris, Flammarion

Banet-Weiser, S. (1999) The Most Beautiful Girl in the World, Berkely: University of California Press

Boone, S. (1986) Radiance from the Waters, New Haven, CT, Yale University Press

Cooper, Sue Ellen. (2004) The Red Hat Society, New York, NY, Warner Books

Danforth, L. (1982) The Death Rituals of Rural Greece, Princeton, NJ, Princeton University Press

Huyler, Stephen. (1985) Village India. New York, Harry N. Abrams

ILLUSTRATIONS CREDITS

Cover: Jason Dewey/WorkbookStock.com; 2-3 Jodi Cobb; 4 Joel Sartore; 6-7 Steve Winter; 8-9 Jodi Cobb; 10-11 Maynard Owen Williams; 12-13 Cary Wolinsky;14-15 Jodi Cobb; 20 William Albert Allard; 24-25 Theo Westenberger; 26-27 James L. Stanfield; 28 Karen Kasmauski; 36-37 David Allen Harvey; 38-39 Karen Kasmauski; 40 O. Louis Mazzatenta; 41 Stephanie Maze; 42 Volkmar Wentzel; 44 Jose Medeiros; 45 NGS Image Collection; 46 James L. Stanfield; 47 Bruce Dale; 48 Steven L. Raymer; 50 (Top) Robert Clark; 50 (Bottom) Tomasz Tomaszewski; 51 (Top) Tomasz Tomaszewski; 51 (Bottom) David Alan Harvey; 52 Kiyoshi Sakamoto; 54 Maggie Steber; 58 Steve McCurry; 59 Jodi Cobb; 60-61 Steve McCurry; 62 Carole Devillers; 63 John Scofield; 65 Maria Stenzel; 66 Steve Winter; 67 Richard Alexander Cooke III; 68 George Steinmetz; 69 Jodi Cobb; 70-71 Karen Kasmauski; 72 Raymond Lasserre; 74-75 Howell Walker; 76 NGS Image Collection; 84-85 David Alan Harvey; 86-87 Joanna B. Pinneo; 88 Randy Olsen; 89 Annie Griffiths Belt; 90-91 Sarah Leen; 94 James L. Stanfield; 96 (Top) Aldana Espinosa; Guillermo; 96 (Botttom) Albert Moldvay; 97 (Top) Karen Kasmauski 97 (Bottom) David Alan Harvey; 98-99: Heather Perry; 100-101 Dilip Mehta/Contact Press Images; 102 Elizabeth L. Meyerhoff; 103 Bob Krist; 105 Nicole Bengiveno; 106 Joel Sartore; 107 Maria Stenzel;108-109 Steve McCurry;110 Carole Devillers; 111Paul Chelsey;112-113 Maria Stenzel; 116 Cary Wolinsky;118 Ed Kashi;119 William Albert Allard;120-121 Randy Olsen; 122-123 William Albert Allard; 124 Phil Schermeister; 32 William Albert Allard; 134-135 Robert J. Baylor; 136 Pablo Corral; 137 William Albert Allard; 138-139 Walter Sanders/Blackstar; 140 Joe McNally/Sygma;141 Amos Burg; 142 (Top) Dudley M. Brooks; 142 (Bottom) Frederick Crawford Brown by Tsen Ngi Ngan;143 (Top) Dewitt Jones; 143 (Bottom) Michael Nichols; 144-145 Kiyoshi Sakamoto;148-149 Michael S. Yamashita;150 Randy Olsen; 151 Annie Griffiths Belt;152 Raghubir Singh; 154 Penny de Los Santos;155 Karen Kasmauski;157 James Rhubaar; Pg 158 H. Edward Kim;159 Sisse Brimberg;160 David and Gillian Gillison161 Elizabeth L. Meyerhoff;162 (Top) Gordon Wiltsie;122 (Bottom) Bruce Dale;163 (Top) Karen Kasmauski; 163 (Top) Jodi Cobb;164-165 Joseph Baylor Roberts;166 Todd Gipstein; 167 Jodi Cobb;170 Steve McCurry;171 O.C. Havens;173 Richard Nowitz; 174-175 Robert J. Baylor; 176 Jodi Cobb; 184-185 Paul Chesley; 186-187 Peter Essick;188 Peter Essick;189 Sarah Leen; 190 (Top) James L. Stanfield; 190 (Bottom) Jodi Cobb;191 (Top) Jodi Cobb; 190 (Bottom) Jodi Cobb; 193 NGS Image Collection;194 Alexandra Avakian;195 Peter Essick;198 Jodi Cobb;199 Stuart Franklin; 200 Aldana Espinosa; Guillermo; 201 Cobb; 202: Edward S. Curtis; 204 T.C. Lau; 205 Jodi Cobb; 206 Jodi Cobb; 207 Robb Kendrick; 208-209 Chris Johns; 210 Lavasseur; 211 Adam Warwick. 212 Rudolph Balogh; 214-215 Michael K. Nichols; 217 Jodi Cobb; 218 Chris Johns; 220 Charles O'Rear.

Mother, Daughter, Sister, Bride: Rituals of Womanhood
Joanne B. Eicher / Lisa Ling

Published by the National Geographic Society

John M. Fahey, Jr., *President and Chief Executive Officer*

Gilbert M. Grosvenor, *Chairman of the Board*

Nina D. Hoffman, *Executive Vice President*

Prepared by the Book Division

Kevin Mulroy, *Senior Vice President Publisher*

Kristin Hanneman, *Illustrations Director*

Marianne R. Koszorus, *Design Director*

Barbara Brownell Grogan, *Executive Editor*

Staff for this Book

Karin Kinney, *Editor*

Annie Griffiths Belt, *Illustrations Editor*

Marianne Koszorus, *Art Director*

Jane Sunderland, *Contributing Writer*

Gary Colbert, *Production Director*

Rick Wain, *Production Project Manager*

Rachel Sweeney, *Illustrations Specialist*

Emily J. McCarthy, Lauren Pruneski, *Editorial Assistants*

Manufacturing and Quality Control

Christopher A. Liedel, *Chief Financial Officer*

Phillip L. Schlosser, *Managing Director*

John T. Dunn, *Technical Director*

Chris Brown, *Manager*

Founded in 1888, the National Geographic Society is one of the largest nonprofit scientific and educational organizations in the world. It reaches more than 285 million people worldwide each month through its official journal, NATIONAL GEOGRAPHIC, and its four other magazines; the National Geographic Channel; television documentaries; radio programs; films; books; videos and DVDs; maps; and interactive media. National Geographic has funded more than 8,000 scientific research projects and supports an education program combating geographic illiteracy.

For more information, please call 1-800-NGS LINE (647-5463) or write to the following address:

National Geographic Society
1145 17th Street N.W.
Washington, D.C. 20036-4688 U.S.A.

Log on to nationalgeographic.com; AOL Keyword: NatGeo.

Copyright © 2006 National Geographic Society. All rights reserved. Reproduction of the whole or any part of the contents withoug permission is prohibited.

Library of Congress Cataloging-in-Publication Information

Ling, Lisa; Eicher, Joanne B.

Mother, daughter, sister, bride : rituals of womanhood / Lisa Ling, Joanne B. Eicher. p. cm.

Includes bibliographical references and index.

ISBN 0-7922-4184-3

1. Women--Social life and customs--Cross-cultural studies. 2. Women--Social life and customs--Pictorial works. I. Eicher, Joanne Bubolz. II. National Geographic Society (U.S. III. Title.)

HQ1161.L56 2005

305.4'09--dc22   2005050531

THE BRYANT LIBRARY

3 1490 00450 0183

305.409
L
Ling, Lisa.

Mother, daughter,
sister, bride.

12/05

FROM THE COLLECTION OF
THE BRYANT LIBRARY

WITHDRAWN

DATE

3 1490 00450 0183

10/1   9/13 1 last out 4/09
        3X 3/15 (1/16) (12/17)

THE BRYANT LIBRARY
2 PAPER MILL ROAD
ROSLYN NY 11576

11/21/2005

3X 3/15 (7/21)

BAKER & TAYLOR